THE KARLUK'S LAST VOYAGE

T0033898

THE *KARLUK* IN THE ICE-PACK

" The snow formed a blanket on the ice and later on its melting and freezing cemented the ice snugly about the ship." *See page 26*

THE KARLUK'S LAST VOYAGE

An Epic of Death and Survival in the Arctic, 1913-1916

AS RELATED BY HER CAPTAIN,
ROBERT A. BARTLETT, AND
HERE SET DOWN BY RALPH T. HALE

M. EVANS
Lanham • New York • Boulder • Toronto • Plymouth, UK

M. Evans
An imprint of The Rowman & Littlefield Publishing Group, Inc.
4501 Forbes Boulevard, Suite 200, Lanham, Maryland 20706
http://www.rlpgtrade.com

10 Thornbury Road, Plymouth PL6 7PP, United Kingdom

Distributed by National Book Network

Library of Congress Cataloging-in-Publication Data Available

Printed in the United States of America

Bartlett, Bob, 1875-1946
    The Karluk's last voyage : an epic of death and survival in the Arctic, 1913-1916 / as related by her Captain, Robert A. Bartlett, and here set down by Ralph T. Hale.— 1st Cooper Square Press ed.
        p.cm.
    Originally published: The last voyage of the Karluk. Boston : Small, Maynard and co. 1916
    ISBN 13: 978-1-59077-476-2 (pbk: alk. paper)
    1. Karluk (Ship) 2. Arctic regions—Discovery and exploration. 3. Canadian Arctic Expedition (1913-1918) I. Hale, Ralph T. (Ralph Tracy), b. 1880. II. Bartlett, Bob, 1875-1946. Last Voyage of the Karluk. III. Title.

G670 1913.K37 B37 2000
919.804–dc21   00-06266

INTRODUCTION

In 1928, fourteen years after the *Karluk* was crushed in the Arctic ice and twelve years after the present volume first appeared, a small New York publisher, Blue Ribbon Books, released *The Log of Bob Bartlett: The True Story of Forty Years of Seafaring and Exploration.* The author, Captain Robert A. Bartlett, was not a member of the literati, but an authentic hero, an accomplished polar explorer, and surely the greatest ice captain who ever lived. *The Log* began this way:

> I have been shipwrecked twelve times. Four times I have seen my own ship sink, or be crushed to kindling against the rocks. Yet I love the sea as a dog loves its master who clouts it for the discipline of the house.

Bartlett, whose adventures had given him international renown, then observed that he had often been asked how it felt to face death.

> "That depends," are always my first words in reply. And it does. Because, if the peril is short and swift,

as when a man points a gun at your head, that is one thing. But if you have to cling, half-frozen, for many hours to the rigging of a sinking ship, not knowing which moment may be your last, that is another sort of shiver altogether.

Bartlett was fifty-three years old when he wrote those words. In print and conversation he occasionally lapsed into blarney and corniness more typical of a man decades older, but there is no question that he had been in many extreme situations and come through them—and brought others through as well—by his hard-won knowledge, his immense physical and mental toughness, and his amazing luck.

He was born August 15, 1875, in Brigus, a harbor town in Newfoundland. The Bartletts had been seafarers for generations. His father, uncles, and cousins were ship owners, fishing skippers, and ice navigators. In *Bartlett, the Great Canadian Explorer*, novelist and travel writer Harold Horwood noted that

> Bob spent his childhood among ropes and twines, nets and boats, forests of masts and booms, in a harbor so filled with ships and wharves that his family had actually blasted a tunnel through a huge outcrop of bedrock to give them increased access to the waterfront.

As a child he was sickly and quite frail. "I was very small—almost a dwarf," he remembered. "Tons of linseed meal were used on my chest and tonsils. My, how I suffered!" However, his brother Will recalled, "He beat himself out of it as he grew up. By the time Bob was ten or twelve he was as hard as nails." He was also high-spirited, rambunctious, and recklessly mischievous. Bartlett's father, William, captain of a sealing ship, was a severe Victorian Methodist who did not believe in sparing the birch rod. He beat his son for even trivial transgressions. This distant, cold, disciplinarian father may have instilled some of Bob's toughness.

Bartlett remained an atheist all his life, and until he reached the age of seventeen, he was a constant bed-wetter. Horwood argued that this secret shame, to which he admitted only in his unpublished journals, revealed "a deep-seated insecurity that followed him into manhood. If you could see him alone at night, sleeping on the floor at fifteen or sixteen to escape the disgrace of wetting the bed, you'd see a pathetic figure."

Although his mother was nearly as stern and chilly as his father, Bob felt a lifelong devotion to her. From his grandmothers, both liberal-minded Anglicans, he developed a love of music and books. At the end of his life, living in a New York City hotel room, he was still collecting poetry volumes and attending concerts. It is not surprising that as the *Karluk* slowly sank,

Bartlett alone remained on board, playing records on his Victrola.

At age fifteen, he attended the Methodist College in St. John's, which was, despite its name, simply an advanced high school. He later wrote that he was a poor student and "gave it up after two years as a bad job." In fact, he left because he was still unable to control his bladder at night. "If it hadn't been for that," he noted in his private writing, "I would probably have gone to Mount Allison University." Instead, he went to sea. At first he worked on sealing ships and fishing vessels for his father and other relatives, and later for nonfamilial employers.

By 1898, at age twenty-two, Bartlett was an experienced skipper and navigator with a master's ticket. In the spring of that year, he sailed as first mate on the *Windward*, the flagship of Commander Robert Edwin Peary's expedition to the North Pole. (Bob's uncle, John Bartlett, was the *Windward*'s captain.)

Nearly all the men of the expedition had liaisons with Inuit women. Peary himself took the beautiful Allakasingwah as his common-law wife and fathered several children by her; his American wife accepted the informal bigamy and even became friendly with "Ally," though Peary's supporters tried mightily to keep the scandal quiet. However, commented Horwood, "I have never been able to find evidence that Bartlett himself took advantage of the Inuit custom of sexual hospitality. He appears to have remained celibate in the Arctic—perhaps the only member of the expedition who did."

In this post-Kinseyan age, one wishes to know more about Bartlett's romantic attachments to, and experiences with, women. He certainly seems to have been a heterosexual, was not a misogynist, and enjoyed flirting with women. In his seventies, living in New York, he frequently attended burlesque shows.

In *The Log*, he told how as a young man he had fallen deeply in love with an unnamed woman. They were to be wed but quarreled, and she broke off the relationship. Bartlett expressed gratitude that through his perilous misadventures he had been spared one "misery": "The feeling in the face of death that I was leaving a wife and children behind me. I never got married. I don't think a sea-faring man ought to because women so often break your heart."

It seems an odd comment. It would not be unheard of for an explorer or a sailor of his time to remain single or to marry only late in life. Nor would it be surprising for Bartlett to express the sentiment that a seafaring man ought to remain a bachelor since, if he married, he might be obliged to stay at home and provide for his family or because in dangerous moments his judgment might be clouded and his attention distracted from the crucial tasks at hand by worries over what would become of his wife and children if he were to die. But to hold that a seafaring man ought not marry for fear of a "broken heart"? Was this a romantic pose he struck for his readers, or had he really been so badly hurt that he carried a torch all those years?

✿ ✿ ✿

Peary spent four years in the Arctic and returned to the United States in 1902 without attaining his major objective: reaching the North Pole. On one occasion both his legs became frozen below the knee; as a result he lost eight toes, six of which had to be removed by pliers, the only suitable instruments available in the desolate and primitive Arctic environment. For the remainder of Peary's life he walked only with difficulty and while traveling in the Arctic, he was usually hauled on a sledge. Nevertheless, determined to try for the Pole again and having had numerous chances to take measure of Bob Bartlett, Peary was convinced that Bartlett was the man to get him there. Therefore, he invited Bartlett to help design and to be the captain of a new icebreaker, the *Roosevelt*, the ship destined for the next expedition. Bartlett accepted—only after Peary promised that he would accompany Peary on the final sledge journey to the Pole itself.

Thus, in 1905, Bartlett once more went north. Ultimately, Peary reached the latitude of 87° 6' on this attempt, but the poor condition of his dogs and the near depletion of the food supply forced him to turn back. The expedition returned to Brigus in January 1907, and, while Peary desperately scrounged for money to fund another Arctic expedition, Bartlett undertook a series of seal-hunting voyages. In the spring of 1908, he was in command of the barkentine *Leopard* when she was wrecked on rocks near Cappahayden, Newfoundland.

This was one of the worst moments in Bartlett's life. He felt he had failed both as an explorer and as a seal hunter. Peary rescued him from his depression, and they went north again, setting sail from Oyster Bay, New York, on July 7, 1908. Nearly eight months later, on February 28, Bartlett set out from Cape Columbia, Canada, with eight sledges, fifty-six dogs, and a number of Inuit. Peary followed with another party about a week later. "We were the pioneer party," Bartlett recalled. "Our work was to set the course, break the trail, and gauge the distance for the main party." He and the Inuit cut their way over rough ice and pressure ridges, often progressing at the rate of only a half a mile an hour.

At the end of March, Peary arrived at Bartlett's final camp, which was beyond 87° North and only 150 miles from the Pole. Although Peary had repeatedly promised Bartlett that they would go to the Pole together, now—at the very last moment—Peary ordered Bartlett to go back, choosing instead an able, longtime subordinate, Matthew Henson, and four Inuit to make the final dash with him. In later years Bartlett hid his feelings, but at the time he was bitterly disappointed. He argued and pleaded with Peary. He actually wept and started out alone for the Pole before coming to his senses and, good sailor that he was, doing as he was ordered.

In later years Peary offered various explanations for having broken his promise to Bartlett, but critics would charge that Peary knew he would be unable to reach the Pole. Bartlett was an excellent navigator, unlike Henson, and would have known where he was at all times. Peary could only claim credit for having reached the Pole if Bartlett could not contradict him. Typically, in the long-running, highly charged controversy over whether or not Peary had reached the Pole, Bartlett did not undercut Peary but supported him.

Between 1910 and 1913, Bartlett lectured before learned societies, went sealing, and took millionaire sportsmen on hunting expeditions to Arctic islands.

In June 1913, the famous Canadian explorer Vilhjalmor Stefansson asked Bartlett to skipper the *Karluk*. There is no need to summarize the misadventures and ordeals of the expedition since the reader has Bartlett's compelling account in hand. Readers who wish to know more should obtain the recollections of survivor William Laird McKinlay. After surviving the Arctic, McKinlay fought in World War I and then became a schoolteacher in his native Scotland. For sixty years he corresponded with fellow survivors and compiled a dossier on the expedition. In 1976, at the age of eighty-eight, he published *Karluk: The Great Untold Story of Arctic Exploration*. The book has recently been republished in paperback under the title *The Last Voyage of the Karluk* (which is a bit odd since that was the original title of Bartlett's book, first published in 1916).

Once the *Karluk* was ice-trapped, Stefansson abandoned the expedition to go on his dubious caribou hunt, leaving Bartlett in charge. The expedition's scientists, sophisticated Europeans who had been with Sir Ernest Shackleton in the Antarctic, did not trust Bartlett because he did not look or act like a leader: he wore a sloppy sweater and baggy pants instead of a uniform and had an affable, deceptively casual manner; to them he seemed nothing more than a Newfoundland fisherman. So the men of science went off on their own—and quickly died. They had failed to appreciate Bartlett's Arctic knowledge—in crucial respects a different environment from the Antarctic—or to discern his inner toughness and leadership abilities. When necessary, he could be decisive and fierce, driving men to life-saving tasks and refusing to allow them to give up. "Captain Robert Bartlett saved my life," McKinlay has said, and the other survivors wholeheartedly agree.

During World War I, Bartlett, by then a U.S. citizen, worked for the Army Transport Command, ferrying troops and supplies, mostly from one mainland port to another. The bungling U.S. government bureaucracy that he was forced to deal with, and his desire to be in Europe fighting Germans, depressed and frustrated him. (Two of Bartlett's brothers died in the war.)

Although in *The Log* Bartlett would disingenuously claim to be a lifelong teetotaler, in the years following World War I he fell into a downward spiral of despair and severe alcohol abuse. His increasingly intolerable drunkenness caused him difficulty in finding work as a skipper. Not even wealthy sportsmen would hire him for their hunting expeditions, though they were happy to invite him to stag parties, where he was cheap entertainment. Plied with free food and bootlegged liquor, he would spin his colorful sailor's yarns. At one party he passed out and, upon regaining consciousness, realized that his hosts were laughing at him. They were waiting for his performance to begin. Bartlett left—and gave up drinking.

In 1925, with the backing of a rich friend, he bought a small schooner, the *Effie M. Morrissey*. Over the next twenty years he made many profitable fishing and hunting trips in the ship and undertook twenty Arctic voyages. He collected scientific data and millions of scientific specimens, which he donated to museums (most notably the Smithsonian Institution), adding greatly to our knowledge of the North. There were so many books and magazines piled on his bunk that, in an ironic reflection of his adolescence, he slept on the floor. In the 1930s he wrote a third book (*Sails over Ice*), gave lectures, and managed to stay afloat during the Great Depression.

In 1942, when he was sixty-seven and contemplating retiring from the sea and living on a farm near Brigus, the U.S. government commandeered the *Morrissey* for use in the Hudson Bay and around Greenland. Bartlett's age precluded his being conscripted, of course, but he volunteered to go with his ship, as did his entire crew. In Horwood's estimation, "Bartlett's war years were spent on some of the most arduous voyages of his life. Unlike his private expeditions that began in June and ended early in September, they ran from April until well into October and sometimes into November." He nursed a deep contempt for the career military officers under whom he sailed, and he even doubted that the war was worth fighting. He set his thoughts down in journals and read literary classics—notably Wordsworth's *The Prelude* and *The Excursion*. When not at sea, he lived in a room at the Murray Hotel in New York City. While there, he attended Broadway shows, concerts, operas, and, of course, the burlesque.

In November 1945, Bartlett, who was seventy years old, sailed the *Morrissey* to the Bay of Fundy, then wintered in New York City, slipping once more into his dry dock routine. In April he was still debating whether to retire to a farm or refit his ship and return to the sea when he caught a "spring cold." He refused bed rest, and so he developed pneumonia. In the hospital he joked with visitors and flirted with nurses, but on April 28, 1946, Bartlett succumbed. He was buried in a Brigus churchyard.

Space limitations have prevented my giving a more thorough summary of Barlett's fascinating life. Those wishing to know more about his adventures must turn to his books and articles, the Horwood biography, and the McKinlay volume.

❈ ❈ ❈

On board the *King and Winge*, the ship that rescued the *Karluk* survivors, was a "cinematograph" cameraman. When it was time to board the ship, remembered McKinlay,

> We staggered out across the ice for the last time. We were sure we could walk unaided the three miles to the ship, but the cameraman insisted that each of us should be supported by two of the ship's company. I think it made for a better picture.

More than a decade ago, while researching the *Karluk* tragedy, I managed to locate a copy of the black-and-white footage. After a lapse of so many years, McKinlay's memory had been wrong in at least one respect: each survivor is not shown being supported by two crewmen, but being led to the *King and Winge* by only one. In every case the sailor does not half carry the survivor, but escorts him with a hand on his upper arm, a gesture suitable for assisting an elderly person into church. Then the film cuts to the *Bear* and Robert Bartlett, with his powerful frame, square jaw, and massive, plain face, wearing an eight-point cap and intermittently flashing a wide, hard, wolfish grin.

EDWARD E. LESLIE
Massilon, Ohio
June 2000

CONTENTS

CHAPTER   PAGE

I   THE EXPEDITION AND ITS OBJECTS 1

II   THE VOYAGE BEGINS 10

III   WE MEET THE ICE AND GET A POLAR BEAR . 16

IV   WE ARE FROZEN IN 23

V   OUR WESTWARD DRIFT BEGINS 29

VI   STEFANSSON'S DEPARTURE 34

VII   DRIVEN BY THE STORM 39

VIII   WE DRIFT AWAY FROM THE LAND 48

IX   IN WINTER QUARTERS 59

X   THE ARCTIC NIGHT 71

XI   THE SINKING OF THE KARLUK 83

XII   OUR HOME AT SHIPWRECK CAMP 93

XIII   WE BEGIN OUR SLEDGING 105

XIV   THE SUN COMES BACK 117

XV   THE RETURN OF MAMEN AND THE DEPARTURE OF THE DOCTOR'S PARTY 124

XVI   OVER THE ICE TOWARDS WRANGELL ISLAND . 137

XVII   THROUGH THE PRESSURE RIDGE 150

XVIII   WE LAND ON WRANGELL ISLAND 161

XIX   KATAKTOVICK AND I START FOR SIBERIA . . 171

XX   ACROSS THE MOVING ICE 179

XXI   IN SIGHT OF LAND 194

XXII   WE MEET THE CHUCKCHES 207

CONTENTS

CHAPTER PAGE

XXIII EASTWARD ALONG THE TUNDRA 220

XXIV COLT 231

XXV "MUSIC HATH CHARMS" 242

XXVI WE ARRIVE AT EAST CAPE 253

XXVII WITH BARON KLEIST TO EMMA HARBOR . . 264

XXVIII IN TOUCH WITH THE WORLD AGAIN . . . 280

XXIX WAITING 285

XXX OFF FOR WRANGELL ISLAND 297

XXXI THE RESCUE FROM WRANGELL ISLAND . . . 311

LIST OF ILLUSTRATIONS

PAGE

THE *KARLUK* IN THE ICE-PACK   *See page 26*   *Frontispiece*

THE DRIFT OF THE *KARLUK*   1

THE *KARLUK* IN HER WHALING DAYS . . .   4

VILHJALMAR STEFANSSON   8

THE LEADERS AND THE SCIENTIFIC STAFF BEFORE THE DEPARTURE FROM NOME   10

STEFANSSON AND HIS PARTY LEAVING THE *KARLUK*   36

HAULING THE DREDGE   48

MAKING SOUNDINGS   52

THE SUPPLIES ON THE BIG FLOE   56

PAGES FROM CAPTAIN BARTLETT'S DIARY . .   92

PLAN OF SHIPWRECK CAMP   98

CAPTAIN BARTLETT'S COPY OF THE "RUBÁIYÁT" OF OMAR KHAYYAM   102

THE ICE-PACK   106

LETTER FROM THE DOCTOR'S PARTY TO CAPTAIN BARTLETT   128

MUGPI   142

SHIPWRECK CAMP   144

ANOTHER VIEW OF SHIPWRECK CAMP . . .   148

MAP OF WRANGELL ISLAND   162

FIVE OF THE MEN OF THE *KARLUK* ON WRANGELL ISLAND   180

xxiv LIST OF ILLUSTRATIONS

PAGE

CAPTAIN BARTLETT'S CHART OF THE ALASKAN COAST 204

CAPTAIN BARTLETT'S CHART OF THE SIBERIAN COAST 214

THE NEWS OF CAPTAIN BARTLETT'S ARRIVAL AT
ST. MICHAEL'S REACHES NOME 282

THE CAMP AT RODGERS HARBOR, WRANGELL ISLAND 306

THE RESCUE OF THE PARTY AT WARING POINT,
WRANGELL ISLAND 314

MAKING THE KAYAK ON WRANGELL ISLAND . . 320

THE KARLUK SURVIVORS ON BOARD THE BEAR . 324

THE KARLUK'S LAST VOYAGE

THE DRIFT OF THE KARLUK

THE *KARLUK'S* LAST VOYAGE

CHAPTER I

THE EXPEDITION AND ITS OBJECTS

We did not all come back.

Fifteen months after the *Karluk,* flagship of Vilhjalmar Stefansson's Canadian Arctic Expedition, steamed out of the navy yard at Esquimault, British Columbia, the United States revenue cutter, *Bear,* that perennial Good Samaritan of the Arctic, which thirty years before had been one of the ships to rescue the survivors of the Greely Expedition from Cape Sabine, brought nine of us back again to Esquimault—nine white men out of the twenty, who, with two Eskimo men, an Eskimo woman and her two little girls—and a black cat —comprised the ship's company when she began her westward drift along the northern coast of Alaska on the twenty-third of September, 1913. Years of sealing in the waters about Newfoundland and of Arctic voyaging and ice-travel with Peary had given me a variety of experience to fall back upon by way of comparison; the events of those fifteen months, I must say, justified the prophecy that I made in a letter to a Boston friend, just before we left Esquimault: "This will have the North Pole trip 'beaten to a frazzle.'"

It did; and there were two main reasons why.

One was that the *Karluk,* though an old-time whaler, was not built, as the *Roosevelt* was, especially for withstanding ice-pressure; very few ships are. Dr. Nansen's ship, the *Fram,* was built for the purpose and has had a glorious record in both the Arctic and the Antarctic. The *Karluk,* a brigantine of 247 tons, 126 feet long, 23 feet in beam, drawing 16½ feet when loaded, was built in Oregon originally to be a tender for the salmon-fisheries of the Aleutian Islands. Her duty had been to go around among the stations and pick up fish for the larger ships. The word *karluk,* in fact, is Aleut for *fish.* When later in her career she was put into the whaling service her bow and sides were sheathed with two-inch Australian ironwood but she had neither the strength to sustain ice-pressure nor the engine-power to force her way through loose ice. She had had, however, an honorable career in the now virtually departed industry of Arctic whaling, and was personally and pleasantly known to Stefansson, who had travelled on her from place to place along the Alaskan coast on several occasions during his expeditions of 1906–7 and 1908–12.

The other reason was that the winter of 1913–14 was unprecedented in the annals of northern Alaska. It came on unusually early, as we were presently to learn, and for severity of storm and cold had not its equal on record.

The National Geographic Society had originally planned to finance our expedition, and it was only at the urgent request of the Canadian premier, the Right Hon. R. L. Borden, that the Society relinquished its direction of the enterprise. The Canadian Government felt that since the country to be explored was Canadian territory it was only fitting that the expedition fly its flag and be financed from its treasury.

When I returned from the seal-fisheries to Brigus, my old home in Newfoundland, in the spring of 1913, I found awaiting me a telegram from Stefansson, asking me to join his expedition and take charge of the *Karluk*. I went at once to New York, then to Ottawa for a day with the government authorities and direct from there to Victoria, B. C. It was the middle of May and there was work to be done to get the ship ready to sail in June.

It was an elaborate expedition, one of the largest and most completely equipped, I believe, that have

ever gone into the Arctic. It differed, too, in one
other respect than that of size, from previous
Arctic expeditions, in that its main objects were
essentially practical,—in fact, one might say, commercial. It was in two divisions. The northern
party, under Stefansson himself, was primarily to
investigate the theory so ably advanced by Dr. R.
A. Harris of the United States Coast and Geodetic
Survey that new land—perhaps a new continent—
was to be found north of Beaufort Sea, which is
that part of the Arctic Ocean immediately to the
north of Alaska. "The main work of the party
aboard the *Karluk*"—to quote Stefansson—"was
to be the exploration of the region lying west of
the Parry Islands and especially that portion lying
west and northwest from Prince Patrick Island.
The *Karluk* was to sail north approximately along
the 141st meridian until her progress was interfered
with either by ice or by the discovery of land. If
land were discovered a base was to be established
upon it, but if the obstruction turned out to be ice
an effort was to be made to follow the edge eastward with the view of making a base for the first
year's work near the southwest corner of Prince
Patrick Island, or, failing that, on the west coast
of Banks Island." The *Karluk* was to go first to
Herschel Island, the old rendezvous of the Arctic
whaling fleet and the northernmost station of the

THE *KARLUK* IN HER WHALING DAYS

Canadian Mounted Police. If she should be beset in the ice and forced to drift, it was expected that certain theories about the direction of Arctic currents would be tested, and there would also be opportunity for dredging and sounding.

Both of these main objects were accomplished: Stefansson ultimately found new land and the *Karluk* engaged in an Arctic drift, but neither result was attained in quite the way which was planned when we were getting the ship ready in May and June, 1913. We returned—some of us—rather earlier than we had expected, for we were prepared to be away until September, 1916, and contrary to one of the theories of Arctic currents we did not drift across the Pole to the Greenland shore. Before we started some of the newspaper accounts of the expedition said that the ship might be crushed in the ice; the newspapers are more often correct than they are supposed to be.

Travelling to Herschel Island on the *Mary Sachs* and the *Alaska,* small schooners equipped with gasolene engines, the southern party, under Dr. R. M. Anderson, who had been Stefansson's only white companion on his previous expeditions, was to map the islands already discovered east of the mouth of the Mackenzie River; to make a collection of the Arctic flora and fauna; to survey the channels among the islands, in the hope of establishing trade-routes; to make a geological survey of the coast from Cape Parry to Kent Peninsula and of Victoria Island north and east of Prince Albert Sound, with the primary object of investigating copper-bearing formations; and to study still further the blond Eskimo who had been discovered by Stefansson in 1910.

Peary's attainment of the North Pole in 1909, the goal of three centuries of struggle, enabled the world to give attention to problems unrelated to polar discovery and afforded men an opportunity to realize not only that a million square miles in the Arctic still remained marked on the maps as "unexplored territory," but also that a great deal remained to be done in regions which already had technically been "discovered." Stefansson himself had already proved this. The shores of Dolphin and Union Straits, for instance, had been mapped by Dr. John Richardson as far back as 1826, yet Stefansson, when he found the blond Eskimo there in 1910, was the first white man on record who had ever visited that tribe in all its history. After his return from that remarkable expedition, I had made his acquaintance at a dinner in New York, some time previous to the planning of the expedition of 1913–16, and admired him for his scientific achievements and for his skill and daring in living so long off the country in his many months of exploration in the territory east of the Mackenzie River.

The scientific staff gathered for the expedition was large and well-equipped. Besides Stefansson, anthropologist, and Dr. Anderson, zoologist, it included twelve men who were all specialists. The Canadian Geological Survey detailed four men to our party: George Malloch, an expert on coal deposits and stratiography, who had been a graduate student at Yale; J. J. O'Neill, a mining geologist, whose specialty was copper; and Kenneth Chipman and J. R. Cox, skillful topographers. For studying ocean currents and tides and the treasures that might be brought up from the bottom of the sea we had James Murray of Glasgow, oceanographer, who had worked for many years with the late Sir John Murray, one of the world's greatest authorities on the ocean. Murray had been with Sir Ernest Shackleton on his Antartic expedition and afterwards had been biologist of the boundary survey of Colombia, South America. To study the fish of the Arctic Ocean we had Fritz Johansen, who had been marine zoologist with Mylius Erichsen in East Greenland and had done scientific work for the Department of Agriculture at Washington. As forester we had Bjärne Mamen, from Christiania, Norway, who had been on a trip to Spitsbergen and had done work in the timber-lands of British Columbia. As the study of the Eskimo was one of the most interesting objects of the expeditions we quite naturally had two anthropologists besides Stefansson, one, Dr. Henri Beuchat of Paris, the other, Dr. D. Jenness, an Oxford Rhodes Scholar, from New Zealand. The magnetician was William Laird McKinlay, a graduate of the University of Glasgow, who had been studying in the Canadian Meteorological Observatory in Toronto. The photographer was George H. Wilkins, a New Zealander, who had been a photographer in the Balkan War and possessed mechanical ability. He had a motion-picture apparatus as well as other cameras. In medical charge of the expedition was Dr. Alister Forbes Mackay, who had served in the British navy after his graduation from the University of Edinburgh, and, like Murray, had accompanied Shackleton into the Antarctic. Five of these twelve men, as shall be related, were to lay down their lives in the cause of science during the coming year.

The crew consisted of the following: R. A. Bartlett, master; Alexander Anderson, first officer; Charles Barker, second officer; John Munro, chief engineer; Robert J. Williamson, second engineer; Robert Templeman, steward; Ernest F. Chafe, messroom boy; John Brady, S. Stanley Morris, A.

VILHJALMAR STEFANSSON

King and H. Williams, able seamen; and F. W. Maurer and G. Breddy, firemen. Six of these men —good men and true—were starting on their last voyage. One other member of the crew was added in Alaska,—John Hadley, who signed on as carpenter.

By June 16 we had the *Karluk* outfitted and were ready to leave our berth at the Esquimault Navy Yard. Official photographs were taken and a luncheon was given in Victoria at which Sir Richard McBride, the Premier of British Columbia, on behalf of the people of the province, presented Stefansson with a silver plate, suitably engraved. Stefansson replied and Dr. Anderson and I were also called upon. Later the mayor and aldermen of Victoria visited the *Karluk* and presented us with a set of flags to use when new lands were found.

CHAPTER II

On June 17, cheered on our way by the good wishes of the people among whom we had spent a pleasant month, we left Esquimault for Nome. The trip north was a memorable one for me, for I had never been up the Alaskan coast before and enjoyed the beautiful scenery. We reached Nome July 7 and remained there until the thirteenth, taking on supplies that had come up on the mail-boat *Victoria* from Seattle and transferring supplies from the *Karluk* to the dock for the two other ships of our little fleet.

On July 13, with a farewell salute from the *Bear,* which happened to be in port at the time, we left Nome for Port Clarence, which we reached the next day. All hands immediately set to work getting things in readiness for our voyage into the Arctic Ocean. We blew down the boiler, overhauled the engines, took on fresh water and rearranged our stores and equipment, so that we might know where everything was to be found. The weather was very variable, usually good but very windy at times, with occasional showers. Some of

Wilkins Malloch Beuchat O'Neill   Cox   McKinlay
Mamen McConnell   Jenness
        Chipman
Mackay Bartlett Stefansson Anderson Murray   Johansen

THE LEADERS AND THE SCIENTIFIC STAFF BEFORE THE
DEPARTURE FROM NOME

the scientific staff went ashore and cut grass for use in our boots later on; when a man is wearing the deerskin boots so essential in Arctic work, it is necessary for him to line the bottom with dry grass to act as a cushion for his feet as he walks over the rough sea ice and also to absorb the perspiration, for otherwise his feet would be in constant danger of freezing.

By July 27 we were at last ready to start. Some further repairs were still to be made on the *Alaska* so she remained behind but at three o'clock in the morning we weighed anchor and, accompanied by the *Mary Sachs,* proceeded to sea. Besides the officers and crew we had on board the *Karluk,* Stefansson and his secretary, Burt McConnell, with Murray, Mamen, Malloch, Jenness, Beuchat, McKinlay and Dr. Mackay. We had also a white dog-driver who left us at Point Barrow.

As we were steaming along in the forenoon, about a mile and a half offshore, abreast of Tin City, I saw a rowboat coming towards us, making signals to attract our attention. We altered our course to meet her and when she came alongside we found that she had brought us a message for Stefansson, which had been telephoned from Teller to Tin City. It proved to be from an aviator named Fowler who was then at Teller with his aeroplane; he asked permission to bring his ma-

chine on board the *Karluk,* accompany us for a
while and later on fly from the ship to the shore.
The *Karluk's* deck was already pretty well
crowded with dogs, sledges, sacks of coal and other
gear, and Stefansson finally decided that it would
be impossible to grant the request.

About two o'clock in the afternoon we had Cape
Prince of Wales a-beam on the starboard side and
shaped our course to round the shoal off the cape.
There was a strong westerly wind blowing. By
this time the *Mary Sachs* was hull down astern, so
we put about and went back to see if everything
was all right with her. When we left Port Clarence we had put Wilkins on board the *Sachs* to run
her engine, on account of the temporary disability
of her own engineer and now, as we came near
enough to exchange words, we found that the engineer was feeling well enough to perform his
duties, so we lowered a boat and transferred Wilkins to the *Karluk* again.

With the *Sachs* keeping in shore we proceeded
on our way. The wind began to blow harder and
veered to the northwest, bringing in a dense fog
and a rising sea and making it necessary to put
the ship on the starboard tack, reaching towards
the Siberian coast. We continued on this course
the rest of the day and until well after midnight;
then the wind veered round to the west again and

the sea moderated, but the fog continued. At 2
A. M. on the twenty-eighth our steering-gear gave
out but fortunately we soon had it repaired. At
eight o'clock we reefed her and headed towards
the American shore. The fog still hung low and
thick but there were occasional gleams of sunshine.
We were now steaming through Bering Strait,
across the Arctic Circle, and had twenty-four
hours of daylight.

Finally, at four o'clock on the morning of July
30, the fog began to lift and by eleven it was fine
and clear again, with a strong north-northeast
wind. The *Sachs* was nowhere to be seen; in fact
the *Karluk* did not see her again. We were now
close to Cape Thompson, steaming towards Point
Hope. At ten o'clock in the evening we dropped
anchor off Point Hope, near the Eskimo village.
The Eskimo in their skin-boats and whaleboats
came out to meet us, to trade dogs, boats, furs and
sealskins. About midnight we moved nearer to
the land, and early in the morning Stefansson went
ashore to continue the trading and make arrangements for the services of Panyurak and Asatshak,
two Eskimo boys eighteen or twenty years old, who
also went by the names of Jerry and Jimmy and
were good dog-drivers and hunters. Stefansson
had lived so many years with the Eskimo of Alaska
and the Mackenzie River region, that he knew them

personally, men, women and children, from Point Barrow east along the northern coast, as well as I knew the Eskimo of Whale Sound on the Greenland coast, that little tribe of Arctic Highlanders, numbering only about two hundred and forty, from whom we chose the Eskimo that accompanied us on the *Roosevelt* to Cape Sheridan and played so important a part in the attainment of the North Pole. Later in the morning of the thirty-first, we weighed anchor and steamed around to the north side of Point Hope, where we did more trading, and then proceeded on our way up the coast. By noon we had Cape Lisburne a-beam and shaped our course for Icy Cape, to go about ten miles outside of Blossom Shoals, a dangerous reef off Blossom Point, which has always been dreaded by mariners. Our scientists were busily engaged in writing letters, to be mailed at Point Barrow and taken back on the *Bear* which calls there once a year, usually in August.

Thus far our progress all along had been satisfactory. Early on the morning of August 1, however, we began to note indications of the presence of ice on our weather side. The water began to get smoother, and when we tested its temperature by hauling up a bucketful at intervals, as the day wore on, we found it dropping steadily, until it reached thirty-nine degrees; the water changed color, too, becoming dirtier. Finally in the afternoon we could see the ice plainly on our port bow. We had seen the "ice-blink" for some time before; now the ice itself hove in sight about two miles away, with some larger pieces scattered here and there among the floes. I learned afterwards that up to a few days before we should have had clear water all the way to Point Barrow. The ice curved in towards the shore, so that we had to change our course; we had been steaming parallel with the land but now we had to head towards shore or else run the danger of being caught in the ice. About midnight our progress was still further barred and we had to turn around and steam back to windward for a mile or so to keep in the open water, for the strong north wind was driving the ice towards the land. The next day the wind changed and blew off the land; this started the ice off shore and we were able to move eastward, but soon the offshore breeze died down and we had to turn back again. Finally in the afternoon we made another attempt, with some success; we were gradually nearing Point Barrow.

CHAPTER III

While we were steaming along off Point Belcher, about seventy-five miles to the southwest of Point Barrow, I was in the crow's nest, which on the *Karluk* was situated at the foretopgallant-mast, conning the ship through the broken ice, when through my binoculars I saw a polar bear about three miles away on the level floe. This was a welcome sight, for the meat would be an addition to our current food supply and the hide useful in several ways. There was no wind, so the bear did not scent us. At first we could not go towards him because the ice was too closely packed,—in fact at times we had to steam away from him to follow the open lanes of water—but finally we managed to get headed in the right direction. When we got within a few hundred yards of him he spied us and promptly went into the water. That was just what I wanted; if he had stayed on the ice he would probably have started to run and as he could run much faster than the ship could steam he would probably have got away from us.

With the bear in the water I now worked the

16

ship to keep between him and the ice and as polar
bears, though they are good swimmers, do not often
dive, I knew that with ordinary luck we should get
him. Shouting to the mate to keep an eye on him I
ran down the rope-ladder from the barrel and
rushed forward to the forecastle-head with a Winchester in my hand. Some of the other members of
the expedition, too, hearing the word bear, grabbed
their rifles and blazed away at him. Every one was
pretty much excited and for a few moments the bear
seemed possessed of a charmed life. At last my
second shot hit him in the back and my third in the
head. This finished him; he keeled over and
floated. We lowered a boat, towed the bear to the
side and hoisted him on board; then the Eskimo
skinned him. He was old and, as he had on his
summer coat, his hair was sparse and yellow and
of no great value. The Eskimo cut up the meat
for dog food; we should have used it ourselves if
we had not just obtained a large supply of fresh
meat at Nome and Port Clarence.

The skin of this old bear had something of a history. The Eskimo stretched it on a frame and
hung it up in the rigging for the wind and sun to
cure it. I had a pair of trousers made from the
softest part of the skin, which later I gave to Malloch. From the remainder I had a sleeping-robe
made which I used on the ice from the time the

ship sank until I reached the coast of Siberia. There I traded it for a deerskin which I afterwards gave to a native at East Cape. The skin of the polar bear makes the best sleeping-robe for Arctic use and the skin of a young bear is also the best for trousers, because it will wear the longest and, furthermore, the hair will not fall out, in spite of the brushing and pounding you have to give it to get rid of the snow that will cling to it after the day's march.

Some time after we got this bear, I saw another one from the crow's nest. We were going away from him, however, and getting along pretty well, so I hardly felt it wise to stop for him. Occasionally we saw walrus asleep on the ice.

August 3 the wind again veered to the southwest, pushing the ice on shore and jamming the ship in it so that we were unable to make any progress. We were about four miles off the Seahorse Islands. Here we found a current running to the eastward parallel with the shore and we began to drift with this current in an easterly direction which was the way we wanted to go. By eleven o'clock we had reached a point about two miles from shore and twenty-five miles southwest of Point Barrow.

The early presence of ice on this coast convinced us that all was not to be plain sailing on our voyage to Herschel Island and that it behooved us to save every hour possible. With this in mind, Stefansson now decided to go ashore and make his way to Point Barrow on foot. He would need at least a day there to obtain furs for our use and he could have his work all done by the time we reached there. Accordingly, at eleven o'clock, he took the doctor and a couple of Eskimo, with a dog sledge, and went ashore over the ice, the Eskimo and the dog-sledge returning late in the afternoon. It was summer and there was no snow or ice on the land so by walking all night in the continuous August daylight, Stefansson and the doctor reached Point Barrow in the morning.

By the sixth, usually drifting only a few miles a day but occasionally getting clear of the ice for a while to go ahead under our own power, we had reached a point about a mile from shore off Cape Smythe, which is only a few miles from Point Barrow. At midnight Stefansson returned from Point Barrow, bringing with him some new members of the expedition: an Eskimo family of five, consisting of Kerdrillo or Kuralluk, a man about thirty-five years old, his wife Keruk, about twenty-eight, and their children, a girl of seven who went by the name of Helen and a baby called Mugpi not much over a year old; an Eskimo named Kataktovick, between eighteen and twenty years old, who was already a widower, with a baby girl whom he

had left with his mother; and John Hadley, a man
between fifty-five and sixty years old, who for a long
time had been in charge of the whaling station at
Cape Smythe owned by Mr. Charles Brower, the
proprietor of the store at Point Barrow. Mr.
Hadley had resigned his position to go east to
Banks Land and establish a trading-station of his
own, chiefly to get foxskins by barter with the
Eskimo. As we were on our way to Herschel
Island, now was Mr. Hadley's chance to get to his
destination, for at Herschel Island he could be
transferred to the *Mary Sachs* or the *Alaska,* when
they reached there, and so go east in the direction
of Banks Land with the southern party. In the
sequel Mr. Hadley, who, as I have already mentioned was put on the ship's articles as carpenter,
proved a very valuable addition to the party, but
he did not get to Banks Land.

While we were at Cape Smythe, the white dog-
driver who had accompanied us from Port Clarence asked for his discharge and went on shore.
We sent our mail ashore to be taken to Point Barrow. As a result of our trading with the Eskimo
here we obtained altogether three skin-boats, two
kayaks and a number of sealskins for boot-soles.
The Eskimo Kerdrillo brought his three dogs to
add to our own.

There is a wide difference between the skin-boat

and the kayak. The former is shaped not unlike
an ordinary rowboat and is large enough to hold
from ten to twenty persons. Over the framework
are stretched sealskins, sewed together with deer
sinew, which makes the boat water-tight. The skin-
boat will stand a lot of wear and tear. The kayak,
on the other hand, is small, pointed at both ends
and completely covered over except for an opening in the middle, where the single occupant sits.
The kayak is used for hunting and as it is small
and light can be easily placed on a sledge and
drawn over the ice.

During the early morning of August 7 the ice
began to move us eastward around Point Barrow,
where we met a current from the southeast and began to drift towards the northwest, until by the
next day we were ten miles from land. We were
still unable to use our engines and the ice was
closely packed, though it had been smashed and
pounded by its constant impact against the
grounded floe along the shore. While we were
still jammed in the ice we took the opportunity of
filling up our tanks from a big floe not far away
on which there was a lake of fresh water where the
sun and the rain had melted the ice.

Early on the ninth we got clear of the ice at last
and steamed eastward along the shore, free for the
first time for many days. The ice was closely

packed outside of us but near shore there was open water and we had little difficulty in making our way along. Navigation was precarious on account of shallow water, but we used the hand lead-line constantly. On the tenth while rounding a point of ice we got aground for two hours, but the use of the anchors and engines enabled us to back off into deep water again. The bottom was soft with the silt carried down the rivers in the spring freshets and the ship sustained no damage. We now made pretty steady progress to the eastward, though the ice constantly threatened our path, and by the eleventh had reached Cross Island, about half way from Point Barrow to Herschel Island.

CHAPTER IV

It was clear by this time that there would be no chance this year to reach new lands to the north by direct voyaging and that we should be lucky if we succeeded in winning our way through to Herschel Island before the ice closed in for the winter. By the afternoon of the eleventh we managed to get as far east as Lion Reef. Here we tied on to a grounded floe to hold our gain and take advantage of our next chance to go east. Between Lion Reef and the mainland a few miles away ran a current which set the ice moving smartly in all directions, but unfortunately we drew too much water to venture into those shallow lanes.

I took the opportunity afforded by our pause to examine the stem of the ship and found that by contact with the ice two of the brass stem-plates were gone and several bolts loosened in those that remained.

Whenever we were stationary in the ice, Murray, the oceanographer, would use his dredge. He had been doing this in fact all along the coast, ever since we were off Blossom Shoals. At this time he used a dredge which he had brought with him; later on he used dredges made by our engineers.

The dredge consisted of a rectangular frame, two feet by three, made of four iron rods two inches wide by half an inch thick, welded together at the corners, with a bag about two feet deep securely fastened to this framework. The bag was made of cotton twine in a two-and-a-half inch mesh; it narrowed towards the bottom. Sometimes cheese-cloth was placed inside the bag to catch the animalculæ. A rope was fastened to the middle of one side of the framework so that, when lowered to the bottom of the sea, the framework would maintain an upright position, with the bag extended out behind it.

When Murray got ready to use the dredge he would get over the rail of the ship, which was only four feet above the surface of the ice, go to the edge of a lead and find out the depth of the water by the hand lead-line; then he would lower the dredge, put the rope on his back and walk along the edge of the lead, dragging the dredge behind him. He could handle it alone up to a depth of twenty fathoms; beyond that he had to have help, which we all of us gladly gave. I do not believe that dredging was ever done in that part of the Arctic before. Before we got through we had brought up a good many specimens which were entirely unknown to Murray, and others, such as coral, which we had hardly expected to find in that neighborhood.

While we were tied up off Lion Reef, I sent out a boat to make soundings; the report was so promising that we started on our way again, on the morning of August 12, steaming through the loose ice and keeping as near shore as possible. The ice moved according to the direction and velocity of the wind, to which its irregularities afforded plenty of sail-like surfaces. The wind had been northwest, keeping the ice packed towards shore; it now veered round to the southwest and loosened the ice to the northeast, outside of the reef. We steamed along through the open water and because the ice near the shore was closely packed, we were driven farther off shore than I liked. We had to follow the open lanes, however, and go where they led.

About eight P. M. we were stopped by a large, unbroken sheet of ice. This was very similar to the ice which I have seen in Melville Bay on the west Greenland coast; it was part of the past season's ice. Seldom over a foot thick, it was honeycombed with water-holes; the *Roosevelt* could have ploughed her way through it but the *Karluk* was powerless to do so.

We were now half way across Camden Bay, about

fifteen miles west of Manning Point, about where
Collinson, in the *Enterprise,* had spent the winter
of 1853–4. We had come about 225 miles from
Point Barrow, considerably more than half the distance to Herschel Island. It seemed at the moment as if we should be able to get through for the
rest of the way. As events proved, however, this
was our farthest east, for the next day, August
13, the open water closed up astern, the ice came together all around us and held the ship fast. There
was scarcely any wind and consequently no movement of the ice.

The next day conditions remained the same.
We tried to force our way towards the land but
failed and could do nothing but wait. For several
days there came no appreciable change either in
weather or in our position until on the eighteenth we
had a heavy snowstorm all day, which was just what
was needed to make assurance doubly sure; the
snow formed a blanket on the ice and later on its
melting and freezing cemented the ice snugly about
the ship so that she was made almost an integral
part of the floe itself. The weather was perfectly
calm but so dull and hazy that for several days we
could not see the shore. Finally on the twenty-
first we had a fine, clear day and about thirty miles
south of where we lay, could see the snow-capped
summits of the Romanzoff and Franklin Moun-

tains, the northernmost range of the Rockies, the backbone of the continent.

There was very little alteration in the ship's position until August 26 when, with a light north wind, the ice moved a few miles to the westward, carrying us with it. The next day we had a heavy snowstorm with wind from the east and we moved still farther west; the next day we drifted westward again, and the next and the next, and for a good many days, sometimes a knot an hour, sometimes faster, parallel to the land but six or seven miles away from it. At times we could see lanes of open water, but they were always too far way for us to reach with our imprisoned vessel. Yet nearer the land the water was open and, so far as we could tell from where we were, no ship would have experienced much difficulty in making her way along there in either direction. If we had used all our dynamite we could have broken a pathway for about a quarter of a mile but no farther and, as the open water was much farther away than that, there was obviously no use in trying the experiment.

Meanwhile, by August 22, Stefansson had decided to send Beuchat and Jenness ashore, to make their way eastward and join the southern party in the event of our not getting any nearer Herschel Island. In fact, besides the two anthropologists,

McKinlay and Wilkins, also, could properly be
regarded as passengers aboard the *Karluk;* their
apparatus, however, was too heavy for safe transportation to the shore over the ice as it then was,
loose and shifting.

All hands busied themselves in getting Beuchat
and Jenness ready for their journey. On account
of the precarious nature of the young ice, however,
which was making in the leads towards the land
and between the older floes but was not yet altogether dependable, the start was not made until
the twenty-ninth. They got away about eleven
A. M. with one sledge and seven dogs and a supporting party consisting of Wilkins, McConnell
and the doctor and three Eskimo, two of whom
were to return to the ship with the sledge and dogs
and the supporting party. On the sledge they
carried a skin-boat in which Beuchat and Jenness
might proceed to Herschel Island, where they
would find plenty of food, whether the *Mary Sachs*
and the *Alaska* succeeded in reaching there or not.
The whole project went awry, however, because
the party had gone scarcely a mile and a half from
the ship when the skin-boat was damaged, as the
sledge bumped along over the rough surface of the
ice, and when Stefansson went out to investigate he
ordered the whole party back to the ship again.

CHAPTER V

The problem of laying in an adequate supply of fresh meat for the winter, for our dogs and ourselves, was now beginning to be a serious one. Long before this we had expected to be at Herschel Island but now with a fairly steady drift in the opposite direction it was evident that we should hardly be able to go the rest of the way before the ice broke up the next summer. This meant a whole year's delay in carrying out the purposes of the expedition, all on account of the unexpectedly early setting in of winter, and it meant, too, the unforeseen question of a winter's supply of fresh meat for the thirty-one human beings—twenty-four white men and seven Eskimo—now on board the *Karluk*. Without fresh meat there was always danger of scurvy, that blight of so many earlier Arctic explorers, which later expeditions—notably those under Peary—had been able to avoid by systematic killing of whatever game the country afforded for food.

Our four Eskimo men made daily trips to the open leads to shoot seal; they were only moderately successful, for the seal seemed to be rather scarce. Occasionally, too, we got a taste of duck-shooting as the birds came flying along the open water on their way south for the winter.

On Thursday, September 11, Wilkins, Mamen and I went out to an open lead after ducks. We took with us one of the three Peterborough canoes which we were bringing along to be transferred to the southern party at Herschel Island for use in navigating the small streams east of the Mackenzie. Dragging the canoe on a sledge to the edge of the lead, we made tea and had a little lunch, and then paddled up the lead in search of ducks. As we went along, we saw several seal and shot one which sank before we could get it.

Soon we saw the birds flying along the landward edge of the ice. We crossed over and I climbed out of the canoe into a kind of natural "blind" formed of the raftered ice, while Mamen and Wilkins paddled along towards the bottom of the lead. They met a good deal of newly formed ice, less than a quarter of an inch in thickness, which they had to smash with their paddles as they went along. There were plenty of birds near the bottom of the lead but the smashing of the ice disturbed them so that Mamen and Wilkins had to turn back and paddle over in my direction, picking out of the

water as they came along a few ducks that I had
shot from my blind.

The wind had changed; the ice began to close up
and thin ice began to form in the smaller leads, so
we had to paddle pretty fast to get out into the
open lead without being caught. It was a beautiful sunshiny day and the surface of the water was
so clear and smooth that, although the ship was
fully two miles away from us in the ice, her rigging
was reflected in our lead. We were getting sun-
sets now, with the gradual shortening of the daylight; the sunset was red and brilliant on this particular day, giving the white ice the lovely appearance of rose-colored quartz. We hauled out the
canoe, lashed it to the sledge and left it there for
another day's shooting. Returning to the ship we
found that other members of the party, too, had
brought in some ducks so that among us we had
about fifty birds, a good day's work.

It was on such journeys as this that I first
learned the use of the ski. Mamen was from Norway and had been a famous ski-jumper in that land
of winter sports; he had won many prizes for his
skill. I knew that Nansen, on his journey from
the *Fram* to his farthest north and back to Franz
Josef Land, had used ski and so had Amundsen on
his journey to the South Pole, but with Peary we

had always used snowshoes and I had never had a pair of ski on my feet. Mamen now persuaded me to try skiing and a rare sport I found it. Not far from the ship we had a ski-jump, made by filling in an ice-rafter about thirty feet high with blocks of ice; we covered it with snow and then over all splashed water which froze and made the surface very slippery. We would climb up the back of the jump on the soft snow by side-stepping on our ski and then coast down the front. Mamen showed me how to do the telemark swing.

We would walk out to the water-holes on ski, with a shotgun apiece, in search of ducks. For several days we had no luck because many of the water-holes where the birds were in the habit of resting in their flight were frozen over. Finally on the fifteenth we went out again and did somewhat better. When we shot any birds, however, the young ice that formed in the leads made it difficult to get them. We would then break off a piece of ice large enough and thick enough to hold us and, standing on it as on a raft, push along with our ski-poles and work around to pick up the birds. The ice we pushed through was perhaps a quarter of an inch thick, and we would break it ahead as we went along.

Salt water does not freeze so easily as fresh water, on account of the salt, but when it does freeze the ice is much tougher and less brittle than fresh-water ice. A man breaking through fresh-water ice fractures a considerable surface; in the case of salt-water ice the hole he makes is just large enough to let him through. Salt-water ice bends and buckles but will still bear you when fresh-water ice of equal thickness will break at once. Sometimes we would find the ice too heavy to push through and once when this happened and we had to go back and get a boat into the water we found that during our absence the gulls had eaten the duck we had shot.

All this time, of course, we kept up the regular ship's routine. The darkness was coming earlier in the afternoon as the weeks went by and by September 17 we had to light the lamp for our six o'clock supper. Already, on the fourteenth, we had put the stove up in the cabin. The days were usually cloudy and the engine-room and the galley-stove did not supply quite enough heat to warm the cabin, though in our skiing trips we found it still comfortable in rubber-boots, sweaters and overalls.

CHAPTER VI

For several days the ship had remained stationary,—that is, the ice had shown no signs of movement, and the weather had been generally calm. The Eskimo were becoming more successful in shooting seal for our fresh meat supply, which we kept in a kind of natural refrigerator that we had made by scooping out a hole in the ice not far from the ship. With the ship now apparently securely fixed for the winter, however, Stefansson came to the conclusion that it would be a good thing for some one to go ashore and get game.

He talked the matter over with me at some length on September 18. Kerdrillo was the only one of the Eskimo who had had any experience at deer-hunting and he knew a good deal about the country to the back of us. In fact he was more familiar with land hunting than with ice-travel. I had shot plenty of caribou in Grant Land and Ellesmere Land, as well as in Newfoundland and elsewhere, and volunteered to go, but Stefansson was the only one on board who not only knew how to hunt caribou but also was fully acquainted

34

with the country. He had shot caribou in 1908 and 1909 along the shore from Cape Halkett to Flaxman Island and was not only familiar with all the fishing and trapping places of the Eskimo, not to be easily found by a newcomer to the region, but also knew every Eskimo there personally and might be able to buy fish and meat from them. He might even get some of the Eskimo families to join the expedition, the men as hunters and the women as seamstresses to make fur clothing for the ship's company to wear during the winter which was now upon us. He had heard at Point Barrow that the carcasses of two whales had come ashore at Harrison Bay; these would make good food for our dogs. He decided, therefore, that the task logically devolved upon him. Plans were accordingly made for him to go ashore on the twentieth. We were off the mouth of the Colville River at this time, having drifted half way back to Point Barrow since reaching our farthest east the middle of August.

On the morning of the twentieth I was up early and got things together for the shore party which, besides Stefansson, consisted of Jenness, McConnell and Wilkins, the two Point Hope Eskimo, Jimmy and Jerry, with two sledges and twelve dogs. For supplies they took two Burberry tents, a stove with piping, two axes, a dozen candles, four

gallons of alcohol, a box of dog-biscuit, six tins of
compressed tea-tablets, ten pounds of sugar, a
supply of matches, three sleeping-bags, sheepskin
sleeping-robes, two pieces of canvas for tents, four
slabs of bacon, ten pounds of lard, one hundred and
twenty pounds of fish, twenty pounds of rice, a
box of tinned beef, five pounds of salt, a case of
Underwood man-pemmican (we had two kinds of
pemmican, one for men, the other for dogs, equally
palatable and nourishing) fifteen pounds of chocolate, a box of ship's biscuits or "pilot bread," a
Mannlicher rifle and a shotgun, with ammunition,
six seal-floats and a camp cooking-set.

We all had luncheon together as usual. There
was nothing out of the ordinary about the trip that
was about to take place. Stefansson expected to
be back in about ten days and there seemed no
reason to suppose that the ship would not remain
where she was until the next summer brought a
genuine smashing-up of the ice and freed her. We
all went out on the ice, however, to see the shore
party off and Wilkins took some moving pictures.

Before he started, Stefansson left me the following formal letter of instruction:

C. G. S. *Karluk,* Sept. 20, 1913.
Dear Captain Bartlett:
    On the trip for which I am leaving the *Karluk*
to-day, I expect to make land on the largest second

Stefansson

STEFANSSON AND HIS PARTY LEAVING THE *KARLUK*

from the west of the Jones Islands (Thetis Island).
If the ice is strong enough I expect to cross thence
to near Beechey Point to hunt caribou; if feasible
I may go on to the mouth of the Itkuilik River,
known to the Eskimo as Itkilhkpe, to see if fish
can be purchased there from the natives. Should
the *Karluk* during our absence be driven from her
present position it will be well for you so soon as
she has come to a stop again, and as soon as it
appears safe to send a party ashore, to erect one or
more beacons, giving information of the ship's location. If she goes east, the beacons should be
erected on accessible islands; if west they should be
at Cape Halkett, Pitt Point, or Point Simpson, to
facilitate the finding of the ship in fog or a blizzard
by our party coming from shore or by hunters who
are overtaken by thick weather while away from
the ship. It will be well to have established four
lines of beacons, running in the four cardinal directions from the ship to as great a distance as practicable. There should be some arrangement by
which these beacons indicate in what direction the
ship is from each of them. And some of them
should have the distance of the ship marked upon
them. These beacons need not be large, but should
not be over 100 yards apart to be of use in thick
weather. Flags or other fluttering things should
not be used, for bears might be scared away by
them. On days when an on-shore wind is blowing
it might be desirable that Dr. Mackay run lines of
soundings out in various directions from the ship.
If it becomes practicable send off Malloch and
Mamen for surveying purposes. McKinlay should
accompany them for the purpose of establishing
magnetic stations in connection with Malloch's
survey, Malloch locating the stations for McKinlay so as to save unnecessary duplications of in-

CHAPTER VII

DRIVEN BY THE STORM

All day long on both September 21 and 22, it was dull and cloudy and the barometer was falling steadily, so I was not surprised at daylight September 23 to find the wind blowing from the east forty miles an hour. McKinlay's anemometer was seeing active service at once. I noticed that the Eskimo seemed very uneasy and made frequent visits to the dredge-hole, where we were in the habit of using the hand lead-line to detect movements of the ice; whenever the ice moved we could feel the lead coming with us. After breakfast I began to visit the dredge-hole myself more often than usual. At quarter of ten I was there and felt no drift but at ten, while I had the line in my hand, the lead started to go. Kerdrillo and Kataktovick were near me; handing them the line I asked them what they thought; they instantly replied that we were moving. Immediately I had everything that we had placed on the ice taken aboard again, including the sledge and the canoe which we had used in our duck-shooting, for it seemed likely that the ice would eventually break up. Towards afternoon it began to snow and soon a blizzard was in full blast.

On the twenty-fourth the storm moderated and the sun came out for a short time. The temperature was mild and there was a good deal of water to be seen to the northeast. The Eskimo resumed their hunting and killed three seal. The rate of drift was about two miles an hour; this increased somewhat in the afternoon, when the wind freshened. Sometimes the ship would appear to be in a vast floating island of ice, with water on every hand but too far away for us to reach even if we could have made our way through the solid mass in which we were frozen.

The next day, September 25, the gale, which had sprung up again, continued with unabated violence and the air was filled with snow. The season was wearing on towards the time of unbroken darkness and there were several hours now in the twenty-four when it was intensely dark. The nights were moonless and starless, for the air was filled with blinding snow.

All about us we could hear the ice tearing and grinding. The water through which we were drifting was comparatively shallow and there was danger not only from the great fragments of the floe, which turned up and toppled over and over, but also, and chiefly, from the heavier floes which occurred here and there and had protruding edges, submerged and hidden, like the long, underwater arm that ripped the side out of the *Titanic*. Every moment the *Karluk* was in danger of being tossed up on one of these heavy floes and left stranded, to break up like a ship wrecked on a beach, or of being flung against the ice bodily like a ship thrown by wind and waves against a cliff. At any moment, too, the ice-floe might smash up and release her to the peril of being crushed by the impact of the floating fragments. We all slept with our clothes on—when we slept at all—and kept the boats loaded with supplies, ready to be lowered at an instant's notice.

The drift of the *Karluk* was a much worse experience than the voyage of the *Roosevelt* through Kennedy Channel from Kane Basin into the Arctic Ocean. The waters traversed by the *Roosevelt* were, of course, narrower than Beaufort Sea and they were filled with floating icebergs and floe-ice, but there we had continuous daylight and could see what we were doing and, also, knew definitely where we were headed, whereas in the *Karluk* we might drift in the ice even to destruction, unable to do anything to save the ship. The *Roosevelt*, to be sure, as I have said, was built for pushing through the broken ice but I very much doubt whether, even she, once frozen in like the *Karluk,* would have been able to extricate herself, and how much less effective was the *Karluk* with her weaker construction and less powerful engines. As long as the ice remained frozen solidly about the ship, our chief danger was from the heavy grounded floes; if it broke up, then the fragments were more likely to be fatal to the *Karluk* than they would be to a ship built like the *Roosevelt*.

We were not far from land. In fact from the crow's nest during the day I caught a glimpse of what I took to be Cape Halkett. The next day the storm subsided, conditions improved somewhat, though our drift continued, and by the chart we were not far now from Point Barrow. The hunters were able to go out and the Eskimo brought in three seal.

When we started our drift we had brought the dogs aboard to avoid losing any, because the dogs, of course, were essential to our safety if anything should happen to the ship; we now put them back again on the ice. When aboard ship they were chained in all parts of the deck, wherever we could find room for them, with a leeway of about two feet for each. They had to be kept separate in this way so that they could not get at each other, for when a fight started it was liable to be a fight to a finish. There were about forty of them all told and when they were on board they all barked constantly day and night.

I do not consider the Alaskan dog the equal of the dogs we had with us on the North Pole trips with Peary. I don't know whether contact with civilization has caused them to deteriorate or not. It has certainly had that effect on the Eskimo who, since the coming of the whalers and traders, have not had to depend for their living on the country but go to Point Barrow and the other stations and buy whatever they need, exchanging pelts from the animals they shoot or trap. The dogs that Stefansson took with him on his shore journey on September 20 were obtained from one of the best dog-drivers in Nome. The best of the remaining dogs were none of them so good as the worst of the dogs we had on the North Pole trips. They required more food, could not stand fatigue so well, though they were heavier than the North Greenland dogs, and they were trained for land, not for ice, travel.

When I came to use them later on, I found that they were terrified by the groaning and crushing of the ice and, when they were going over new ice that buckled, they would become frightened and instead of separating would all huddle together for mutual protection; perhaps they were not to be

blamed for this, for though it is all right if you are
used to it, the shifting ice can furnish the un-
initiated with an unlimited number of surprises.
In such times of danger they would not respond
either to the voice or to the whip of the driver.

Driving Eskimo dogs is a hard job at best, for
they seem possessed of the spirit of Satan, himself,
even the best of them. The North Greenland
Eskimo harness their dogs to the sledge fan-wise,
each dog having traces that fasten directly to the
sledge itself, whereas the Alaskan Eskimo harness
the dogs to a long rope, at intervals on either side.
With both methods the dogs get the harness tangled
again and again and then, out of the range of the
whip, they will sit down and blink at the driver in
a way calculated to make him feel like committing
cruelty to animals. They will all of them chew the
harness and free themselves if you give them half a
chance.

We fed the dogs on the *Karluk* on dried salmon
which we obtained at Nome, together with rice and
oatmeal and Indian meal, all cooked together.
As long as we had steam on the main boiler we
cooked the dog-food by letting the steam blow
through a hose leading into a pork barrel filled with
the ingredients. We always served the dogs with
hot food—and it was quite good enough for a man
to eat—and after the boiler was blown down we

cooked it every night in the galley stove. Mr.
Hadley looked after feeding the dogs, and no better man could have been found, for he understood
not only how to feed them but also how important
it was to have them well cared for. Whenever
possible we kept the dogs on the ice, for the free-
dom was good for them. Even then, to prevent
their fighting, we often had to chain them up to
raftered ice.

It is a mistake to think that Arctic weather is
characterized by unvarying cold; on the contrary it
offers radical differences in temperature from day
to day, and the seasons differ greatly from year to
year. We were experiencing an extraordinarily
early and severe winter and yet for the next few
days now the weather was frequently mild and
springlike, with temperatures above the freezing-
point. This does not mean that there was any sudden thaw; the snow fell at intervals and the sky was
overcast but the wind was not bitterly cold as it
became later on in our drifting.

We busied ourselves, as we had from the beginning of the drift, in making preparations to leave
the ship, an event which under the circumstances
was probable at any moment. The Eskimo
woman, Keruk, began making fur clothing for us.
We put all the Jaeger underwear in large canvas
bags placed where they could be reached con-

veniently at once. The whaleboats we provisioned
each for eight persons for twenty days and we put
supplies for a couple of months on deck ready to
be thrown overboard. We fixed up the forward
hold as a carpenter's shop for Mr. Hadley and he
started in to make a Peary sledge.

This was the kind of sledge that I had been accustomed to use on the ice on my various trips with
Peary. He invented it himself, evolving it from
the experience of his years of Arctic work and, in
several important particulars, it was a marked
improvement over the Eskimo sledge. We did not
have the material to make an exact duplicate but
we did the best we could.

The Peary sledge is thirteen feet long over all,
with runners made each of a single piece of hickory
or ash, three inches wide by an inch-and-a-half
thick, bent up by steaming at each tip and shod
the whole length with a steel shoe, like the tire of a
wheel. The bow has a long, low rake and the stern
turns up to make steering with the upstanders true
as the runners slide along. The filling-in pieces are
of oak, fastened with sealskin lashing, and the bed
of the sledge is made of boards of soft wood, lashed
to the filling-in pieces. In loading the Peary
sledge we always put the bulk of the weight in the
middle and left each end light; with its long rake
fore and aft the sledge will swing as on a pivot, so

that when you get into a position where you cannot go ahead you can back the sledge or turn it around and even go stern first if necessary, without lifting it. When, for instance, you come suddenly to a crack in the ice, when travelling with the Peary sledge, you can turn it around or steer it aside. Being constructed with lashings instead of bolts, it is flexible and adapted to the rough going over the sea ice, while in getting through young ice, on account of its turned-up rear end it can be easily dragged back on to firm ice with a rope.

CHAPTER VIII

The last day of September we got another glimpse of the land, seeing distinctly the low shore of Cooper Island, with its Eskimo houses. We were still to the eastward of Point Barrow, drifting slowly along in the pack. Mamen, the doctor and I went out to a ski-jump we had built and in trying a higher jump than usual I heeled over and, instead of landing on my ski, came down with a hard bump on my side. I didn't let the doctor know how badly I was hurt because I didn't want any one to know that I could be such a duffer but I was unable to lift my hand to comb my hair for several weeks.

October came in with a snowstorm and a strong northeast wind which drove us fast before it. On the morning of the first there came a crack in the ice about a foot wide, running east and west, two miles from the ship. It was too far away for us to dynamite our way to it even if it had been a likely lead for navigation and besides when you dynamite ice you must have open water for the broken fragments to overflow into or they will choke up

48

HAULING THE DREDGE

"The dredging and soundings were both carried on through a hole in the ice, which we had made at the stern of the ship." *See page 49*

around you and you are worse off than before. The heavy wind did not allow this crack to remain open more than a few hours.

On the second and again on the third we caught glimpses of the land. On the third the same gale that destroyed part of the town of Nome sent us bowling along to the northwest. Occasionally we saw open water but it was always far away. The weather on the fourth and fifth was delightful, with the temperature up in the forties, and on the fifth we had a beautiful sunset. Mamen, Malloch and I went ski-jumping in the bright sunshine and had a wonderful afternoon of it.

We were now fast drifting to the northwest, off Point Barrow, getting outside the twenty-fathom curve. The farther north we drifted the deeper the water was becoming and the more varied in yield, for we kept up the dredging and now we began to get flora and fauna characteristic of the deep sea, instead of the specimens peculiar to the waters near shore. Our soundings were kept up constantly and showed that we were sliding off the continental shelf, so to speak, into the ocean depths. The dredging and soundings were both carried on through a hole in the ice, which we had made at the stern of the ship. Here we had an igloo—a snow-house—for protection.

Peary had given me the first stimulus to seek

information in the Arctic; he had been the first
to make me feel the fascination of all this sounding and dredging, mapping out the bed of the
ocean, outlining the continental shelf. These
things and the search for new land in latitudes
where man has never set foot before are what appeal to me. Call it love of adventure if you will;
it seems to me the life that ought to appeal to
any man with red blood in his veins, for as long
as there is a square mile of the old earth's surface that is unexplored, man will want to seek
out that spot and find out all about it and bring
back word of what he finds. Some people call
the search for the North Pole a sporting event;
to me it represents the unconquerable aspira-
tion of mankind to attain an ideal. Our *Karluk* drift and its possibilities interested me
keenly, for we were on the way to a vast region
where man had never been; we were learning things
about ocean currents and the influence of the winds
and almost daily were bringing up strange specimens from the bottom of the sea. And I felt sure
that come what might we would get back in safety
to civilization.

For several days we continued our offshore drift
without change, bearing sometimes due north,
sometimes easterly and then again northwesterly
until by the ninth we were about thirty-five miles

from Point Barrow and drifting fast, too fast, in fact, to use the dredge. The depth of the water had by now increased to almost a hundred fathoms.

The afternoon of the ninth Mamen and I were out on our ski, when there came a sudden crack in the ice between us and the ship. Fortunately I was on the watch for just such an event and as soon as I saw the black streak of the open water on the white surface of the ice about a hundred yards away from the high rafter which formed our ski-jump, we started for the lead at top speed. The crack was about ten feet wide at first; the wind was blowing, the snow was falling fast and night was closing in. We had a dog with us and she ran along ahead of us to the lead. The edges of the ice at one point were only about three feet apart and after a wait of five or ten minutes we managed to bridge the gap and get across just in time, but the dog got on another section of ice which broke away and floated off with her.

When I got back to the ship I threw off my heavy ski shoes and went up into the crow's nest. It was stormy and I could not see very far. The crack in the ice was about half a mile away and, as I could see, was closing up. When it closed I feared we should be in for trouble, for the ice was three or four feet thick, and if it should break up all the way down to the ship and get us mixed up in the floating fragments, it might crush the ship in an instant. So I set everybody at work on the jump. For some time we had been placing supplies overboard on a heavy floe not far from the ship and there we already had supplies for several months in case of emergency. When the crack closed up, the ice about 150 yards astern split at right angles into a lane of open water a couple of feet wide.

The thermometer was about zero and there was much condensation in the air, indicating the proximity of a good deal of open water. We had steam up and I decided that if conditions remained the same when daylight came the next morning, so that we could see what we were doing, I would try to get the ship out into the open water and back to the land. I stayed up all night but the next morning I found that all the leads had closed up and through the clear, frosty air no open water was visible in any direction. This proved to be the nearest the open water came to us in all our drift.

The temperature now went down to fifteen below zero and our soundings by the Kelvin sounding-machine gave us no bottom at 270 fathoms. We bent on a reel of 350 fathoms more and got no bottom at 500 fathoms. Then we got the Lucas sounding-machine together and installed it on the

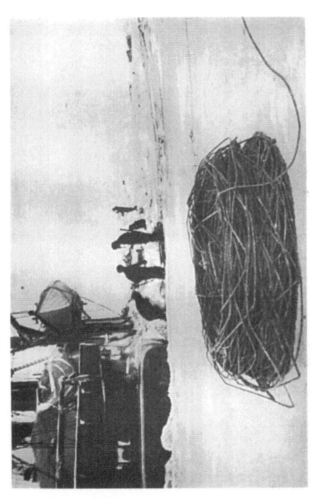

MAKING SOUNDINGS

"We got the Lucas sounding-machine together, and installed it on the ice at the edge of the dredge hole. With this machine on October 11 we got 1,000 fathoms."

ice at the edge of the dredge hole. With this machine, on October 11 we got 1000 fathoms.

The dog that had floated off the day before came
back; this made me happy, because dogs were
valuable to us and this particular dog, whose name
was Molly, was going to have a litter of pups.
All the dogs were now put back on the ice again,
for the leads had all closed up and the danger
appeared to be over for the present.

Our Eskimo seamstress, Keruk, was working in-
dustriously and by now had completed her fifteenth
pair of winter deerskin boots. These are made
from the leg and foot of reindeer that have
been killed during the later fall or winter when
they have their winter coats on, cut up into four
or five strips which are all sewed together to form
leggins, the hairy part inside; the sole is made from
the skin of the ugsug, or bearded seal. Keruk
worked on fur clothing also. She did the cutting
and much of the sewing; some of the men knew
how to sew and they helped, too.

We continued our general drift to the northwest until October 22, when for a few days the
wind shifted and sent us south and east before we
took up our westward drift again. We were then
about twenty-five miles south of where Keenan
Land should have been, according to the map of

the Arctic Region prepared by Gilbert H. Gros-
venor, director and editor of the National Geographic Society, for Peary's book "The North
Pole," a copy of which we had in the ship's library.
We were near enough to have seen Keenan Land
with a telescope from the masthead, on a fine clear
day, but though we kept a constant lookout for it
from the crow's nest, we saw no signs of it whatever.

All this time we continued to get a good many
seal. Most of these were shot by the Eskimo,
whose skill at hunting of this kind far exceeded
that of any other members of the party. We
needed the flesh for fresh meat for ourselves and
fed the skins and blubber to the dogs. The seal
is the one indispensable animal of the Arctic. Its
flesh is by no means disagreeable, though it has a
general flavor of fish, which constitutes the seal's
chief food.

We continued our preparations for an extended
stay in the ice. The ship was now some two feet
lighter than she had been the middle of August
when first frozen in; we had burned a good deal
of coal and had removed coal, biscuit, beef, pemmican and numerous other things from the deck and
also from the hold, sledging them to the heavy floe
of which I have already spoken. This floe was
about half an acre in size and about thirty feet thick,

of blue ice, amply able to stand a good deal of
knocking about before breaking up. We now cut
the ship out of the ice which was fast to her sides,
so that she would ride up to her proper level before
freezing in again.

Whether we were to continue in the ice or get
clear, it was well to have a good supply of emergency stores safe on the ice, because with any ship
at sea there is always the danger of fire. When we
got the *Roosevelt* to Cape Sheridan in 1905 and
again in 1908 we unloaded her at once and put the
supplies on land, building a house of the unopened
biscuit boxes, so that if the ship should chance to
get afire and burn up completely we should simply
have had to walk back to Etah with our supplies
and wait for our relief ship. This experience I
now applied to our situation on the *Karluk*. We
had various coal-stoves on board, one in the saloon,
one in the scientists' room, one in my room, with
fires in the galley and Mr. Hadley's carpenter's
shop and of course in the engine-room, while the
Eskimo had blubber stoves of soapstone in the
quarters we had built for them on deck. Besides
all these stoves we had numerous lamps. To guard
against the danger from fire we had chemical fire
extinguishers and about fifty blocks of snow, distributed wherever there was room for them about
the ship, and in the galley a hundred-gallon tank

with a fire kept going constantly under it to keep the water from freezing. We had a fire-fighting corps, every man of which knew what he must do in case of fire. If fire broke out, the ship's bell would be rung and everybody would seize a block of snow or the fire extinguisher or the buckets near the water-tank, as his duty required, and help extinguish the fire.

Our supplies on the big floe we left at first where we put them. Later on as we got opportunity we built a regular house, with walls composed of boxes and bags of coal, cases of biscuit, barrels and other large articles, with lumber, of which we had put two thousand feet over on the ice, for flooring, scantling for roof and an extra suit of the ship's sails to cover all. We banked it all around with snow for warmth. There was a kind of vestibule of snowbanks and a canvas door so weighted that it would fly to of itself. Later still, in addition to this box-house, we built a large snow igloo.

On the fourteenth for the first time we discontinued the regular nautical routine of watch and watch and instead had a night watchman and a day watchman, all taking turns at the work.

We had a new dredge by this time, a larger and better one, made by Chief Engineer Munro, with a long line, for we were getting soundings of 1200 fathoms. We brought up a brittle starfish on the

THE SUPPLIES ON THE BIG FLOE

"Our supplies on the big floe we left at first where we put them. Later on as we got opportunity we built a regular house, with walls composed of boxes and bags of coal, cases of biscuit, barrels and other large articles."

sixteenth and a spherical-shaped creature unknown to Murray, two or three inches in diameter. Murray had a laboratory which we built on deck for his specimens, and it became a good deal of a museum before it finally went down with the ship.

We got fur clothing enough made by the middle of the month for each man to have an outfit and I had all the skins we had left collected and put in canvas bags. The sailors were busy putting our pemmican in 48-pound packages, sewed up in canvas which later we used for dog harness; canvas is one thing the dogs will not ordinarily chew.

On the twentieth we saw bear tracks near the ship. There had been cracks in the ice and ribbons of open water at some distance from the ship and the Eskimo had continued their seal hunting with considerable success. The dogs, curiously enough, though tethered at various points around on the ice, were not aware of the bear's presence.

Wherever there are seal you will find bear because the bear hunt the seal and live on them. When I was hunting with Paul Rainey and Harry Whitney in 1910 in Lancaster Sound, that historic entrance to the islands and waters west of Baffin Land, I saw a bear creeping along the ice very stealthily. So intent was he that he did not know I was there and I watched him steal up on a seal asleep on the ice. He got nearer and nearer and finally made a spring and landed on his prey. The seal never woke up.

Sometimes the ice would be closed up and our Eskimo would get no seal, or the weather would be bad and the sky overcast, but when the ice parted and the water-lanes opened, if the air was fine, the seal would sometimes swim over to the edge of the floe, put their flippers up and crawl out of the water. Then they would lie out on the ice and sun themselves. After a time, as the sun disappeared and the raw wind came up, they would become cold from staying on the ice and then they would slide back into the water. I have seen seal off the Newfoundland coast that were so sunburned after lying for many days on the ice, blockaded in the bays by the on-shore winds, that they actually cried out with pain when they finally went into the water, and came back on to the ice again at once.

CHAPTER IX

We made another change in our routine October 28, going on to a schedule of two meals a day, breakfast at nine o'clock and dinner at half-past four. Tea could be obtained at one o'clock and at night, before going to bed, any one could have tea or coffee or chocolate. From six o'clock at night to six the next morning whoever was assigned for that night to be watchman was on his rounds, looking after the fires and lights and keeping the water from freezing in the water-tank. All lights except the watchman's lantern were out at midnight. At six o'clock he would wake the cook, who slept in a room off the galley, and after waiting to have his breakfast would turn in, a day watchman taking his place from 6 A. M. to 6 P. M.

For breakfast we always had oatmeal porridge, with condensed milk. This was followed by various things, for we tried to make the menu interesting. We would have eggs, ham, bacon, codfish, sausages, and of course coffee. For dinner we would have canned oysters or clams, shredded codfish from Newfoundland, potatoes (desiccated and

frozen, to be thawed out as we wanted to use them),
carrots, parsnips, spinach, pickles, asparagus,
beans, corn, tomatoes. We always had fresh
meat at least once a day, seal meat or, when we got
any, later on, bear meat. For dessert we had ice-
cream, in all flavors, or sherbet, pies, puddings,
fancy cakes, and earlier had had watermelon and
cantaloupe. At all times we had a great variety
of canned fruits. In fact we were well supplied
with about everything obtainable.

About this time we began putting the clock back
to get the benefit of all the daylight. The men did
not have to get up until breakfast-time but at ten
o'clock they had to be ready for the day's work.
This consisted of sewing canvas, making clothing,
sewing pemmican up in canvas, shifting boxes and
putting things over on the big floe, shovelling snow,
filling up the locker with coal, bringing in fresh-
water ice for melting in the tank, doing various odd
jobs around the ship and fixing up the dredge-
hole.

We had plenty of soap and razors and plenty of
underclothing, so we kept clean. We made it a
rule to shave at least three times a week and to
bathe at least once. Even the Eskimo bathed like
the rest of us. When Kataktovick joined us he
said, "I like my bath." In Nome and St. Michael's the Eskimo have a bath-house where they

can bathe by paying twenty-five cents and they patronize it freely. We had several bath-tubs on the *Karluk*.

On the twenty-seventh, too, we blew down the boiler, drew the water off, disconnected the engines and blew all the water out of the pipes.

At eight o'clock on the evening of the twenty-eighth we were gathered in the saloon, some of us reading, some playing chess, others playing cards, when we were alarmed by a loud report coming from the direction of the bow. In an instant, with practically no interval, we heard another report, from the port quarter. The watchman came in and said there was a crack in the ice at the stem of the ship. I went out and with our lantern we could see what had happened. The ice had cracked at the bow and again about fifty yards away on the port quarter and the ice had opened up for about two feet running in a westerly direction on the port bow. The dogs were separated from the ship by the crack. We made haste to get them on board, together with skin-boats, sledges and sounding-machines, for we were afraid the ice might break up all around the ship. I stayed up all night and had every one standing by for trouble, but again nothing happened, and next morning with a high wind blowing the drifting snow along the surface of the ice and a temperature of twenty-four degrees below zero, we found that the cracks had closed up again. Twice during the day the ice opened again but closed up at once. These cracks were only an inch or two in width.

November began with a renewed violence of the gale and we drifted to the northwest. For the first time we pumped out the hold with a hand-pump in the engine-room. As long as we had steam up we did the pumping with steam from the boiler but now that the boiler was blown down we pumped by hand on deck, but that was a difficult job on account of the cold, so by having a stove in the engine-room which kept the temperature above freezing we found that we could handle the pump to better advantage there.

We built an observatory for Malloch by covering in the bridge with boards and sails with an opening at the top. Malloch had his transit here and was untiring in his efforts to get our position. He relieved me of much of the labor of taking the observations and was a great help throughout. In the afternoon of this first of November we had clear weather for a short time and were treated to a remarkable display of the aurora, one of the few that we had in all our months of drifting and ice travel. During the gale that kept up all day we dragged our dredge and parted the line, so that we had to put on a new dredge. The next day we got specimens of several species, including a number of different kinds of starfish. Our soundings showed that we were drifting in comparatively shallow waters shoaling to 105 fathoms on the first and to 36 on the second. Mr. Hadley and I busied ourselves scraping deerskins, a necessary preliminary to their use in making clothing; the scraping is done to break the vellum, to loosen them up, for when they are hard they do not keep you so warm.

November 4 we found another new animal in the dredge. The soundings now gave us only 28 fathoms. The wind fluctuated in violence all day long, finally settling down to a good-sized gale, with drifting snow. On the seventh open water appeared about two miles from the ship. The Eskimo went out and shot ten seal. I was with them and we saw many more seal out in the water but they were too far away for us.

November 10 was an unusually beautiful day. There was a fresh south wind and the temperature went up to twenty-three degrees above zero; it was almost like a spring day. About three miles from the ship the Eskimo shot six seal. They also got the first bear of our drift, a young one three or four years old, about six feet long, with a good coat. They had been on the lookout for bear, on account of the amount of seal meat they had left on the ice. I intended to give the skin of this bear to the

Boston City Club for its new club-house but we needed it and had to use it for trousers and mittens. Everybody was still wearing American clothes at this time, with deerskin boots.

We had the deck covered with snow about two feet deep to make the ship warm; when the top of the snow became dirty we took off a few inches and replaced it with clean snow. The outside of the ship was banked up and we built a kind of runway from the deck to the ice with walls made of blocks of snow. This made our passage between the ship and the ice easy.

November 11 the sun left us for good; we were now to be without it throughout the twenty-four hours for seventy-one days.

The young Eskimo widower, Kataktovick, came to me the next day and asked me for a fountain pen, to write letters to his Eskimo friends, I presume. Some weeks before he had asked me for a book to read; after a fortnight he brought it back, said that he had read it and asked for some magazines. We had a good many and the pictures were interesting so I let him have them gladly. On this particular day he came into my cabin and saw me writing with a fountain pen. Kataktovick did not ask outright for the pen but simply said that he wanted something to write with. I offered him a pencil but he shook his head and said that was not what he wanted. Then I asked him if the pen was what he wanted. He said it was. I gave him one, as we had a large quantity of fountain pens, and as I gave it to him I thought to myself: "What would Peary say?" To live in the open as they have been accustomed to live is in his judgment the Eskimo's normal existence and not to become dependent on the white man's methods of life. We had a large supply of blank-books on board, in which our scientists jotted down notes and calculations to be afterwards transcribed on the typewriter, and I gave Kataktovick some of these blankbooks from time to time.

The next day we had another wonderful display of the aurora, with brilliant moonlight, which had been lighting up the scene for several days. For a while in the afternoon, as we drifted steadily along, we saw a little of the sun's upper limb. Our latitude was too far north for us to see the real sun at this time of year; it was the distorted sun that we saw, like the mirage which one sees in a desert.

I remember that when I was a boy in the Methodist Academy in Brigus, the town where I was born in Newfoundland, the Anglo-American Telegraph superintendent at St. John's once told us that when he was a young man at Cape Race a certain ship from Europe was expected at a given time but failed to appear. Finally they appar-

ently saw her heading in towards shore, and they
launched a boat and went out to meet her. When
they reached the spot where she was supposed to
be she was not there and did not turn up until some
ten hours later. Her apparent presence was simply a peculiarity of the sea-horizon, a refraction or
distortion.

The Eskimo reported fox tracks a few miles
from the ship and I gave them a dozen fox traps.
The Arctic fox is of a clear white color, his pelt
often whiter than that of the polar bear, which
sometimes verges on the yellow. The Eskimo set
the traps at various points on the ice, fastened
securely so that the foxes would not carry them
away, and on the seventeenth they caught one very
small fox. Mr. Hadley finished the second Peary
sledge. We lost the dredge again on the seventeenth and had to replace it with another one, which
brought up some more specimens new to Murray.
The temperature was only nine below zero but it
was as cold as it is along the Atlantic seaboard in
winter because just now there was much open water
about us, though it was a good many miles away.
On our North Pole trips we had much lower
temperatures than we were now having but felt
the cold less because it remained at the same level
for weeks and was free from dampness because
there were not so many open leads.

On the nineteenth we lost the lead and tube of the Kelvin sounding-machine; the wire kinked and broke, so we had to attach another lead and brass tube. It was a typical Cape Sheridan day, a magnificent morning with hardly any wind and a temperature of nineteen below zero.

Soot had accumulated in the funnel of my cabin stove, so that the fire would not burn, and I determined on the twentieth to adopt heroic measures to get the soot out. The method which I finally hit upon was effective but disturbing. I decided to pour a lot of flashlight powder in the stove, as this would give a quick puff and blow out the soot. I was pouring the powder in, when I inadvertently poured too fast and got too much in. Flash! The door of the stove came off and sailed past my head; if it had hit me it would have killed me. As it was the stove lost its bearings and landed with a tremendous crash against the side of the room, but no particular damage was done—except to the soot.

Murray got a little octopus in the dredge. He had been getting stones, small pebbles at first and then larger ones, almost perfectly round and very smooth. Now, however, he began to get specimens of previously unknown animal life again—eleven different kinds in one day. He was faithful and untiring in his dredging and his work, at which we all helped, was not the kind that had the apparent zest of hunting or exploration in it, but called for patient investigation and, always, hard labor. It was a great pity that we were unable to save the things his dredging brought up.

On the twenty-second my thoughts turned towards Boston and Cambridge, for I knew that this was the day of the Harvard-Yale football game, which I had attended so many times. I wondered who would win and as the afternoon wore on I thought of what must be taking place on Soldiers' Field and of the life and activity in the hotels of Boston the night after the game.

I looked back and remembered some of the things that had happened when I had seen games in the past and wondered when I should see another. I recalled how I went down to New Haven the day before the game in 1910 and went into the country to the Yale headquarters and talked to the team on our North Pole trip of the previous year to take their minds off their troubles. And I remembered, too, how George Borup took the news of the 1908 game when we got our mail for the first time in over a year on our way home in the *Roosevelt* from the North Pole trip in the late summer of 1909. He and MacMillan occupied the same cabin and were eagerly looking over their letters when suddenly Borup began to cry out in

tones of anguish, "Oh, dear! Oh, isn't that ter-
rible! Oh, I can't believe it's true!" until Mac-
Millan was sure that he had learned of the
death of some near relative. Finally when he felt
that he must ask he ventured to inquire the cause of
Borup's mourning and to hope that he had not heard
bad news. "Why, just think!" replied Borup.
"Harvard beat Yale last fall, 4 to 0!" Now, on
November 22, 1913, when the sky cleared to the
south and we were treated to a red glow in that
direction to light up the darkness I wondered if
anything happening in the vicinity of Cambridge
was having its effect on the meteorological conditions.

We had reached nearly to Lat. 73 N. on November 15. This proved to be our farthest north.
After that for a month the winds drove us south
and southwest and then for the rest of our drift
more nearly due west again. We now had a little
relief from the incessant sixty-mile gale which had
been making it intensely cold for a number of days
and on the twenty-fourth the red glow continuing
gave us the effect of a little twilight which enabled
Malloch to read the transit in his observatory without the aid of a lantern. The temperature was
twenty below zero, but the air was so clear and clean
that one could go about out of doors with American
clothes on without discomfort. Just before mid-

night, however, the thermometer began to climb and the barometer to drop, denoting the approach of a storm, and all day long on the twenty-fifth it was a miserable time to be out. We had our work to do, however, and the Eskimo finished banking up the starboard side of the ship with snow to make things as warm and comfortable as possible.

November 27 was Thanksgiving Day in the States but as we were a Canadian expedition we made no observance of the day. My thoughts took another backward glance to the Thanksgiving Days I had spent in Belmont and Winchester and elsewhere, with my good friends of Boston.

The day began early with me because I was awakened from a sound sleep, almost choking to death from the sulphurous fumes of the mess-room stove which I found on getting out of my cabin was smoking badly. Chafe, the mess-room steward, was making heroic efforts to get the fire going to take the fumes off. I told him to take hold of the stove with me and carry it out on deck, which we managed to do.

CHAPTER X

The first few days of December were cold and stormy, with very high winds. I made up my mind that we were in the place where all the bad weather was manufactured, to be passed along to Medicine Hat and thence distributed to Chicago and Boston and points south. We got a little twilight from ten to two on pleasant days, so that the men could see to work out of doors. The health of the party throughout our drift was excellent. Every one had plenty of vigorous, outdoor exercise and slept soundly, though the incessant howling of the wind was not always conducive to a feeling of carefree contentment.

There was considerable pressure early in the month at a point about a mile from the ship, which tossed the ice into rafters, but we did not feel it on board. On the tenth a ribbon of water about a foot wide showed in the ice about two hundred yards from the ship, opening and closing off and on for several days. The temperature was getting pretty cold now, down in the minus thirties, yet the air was clear much of the time and we were not uncomfortable out of doors, even in American clothes. Mr. Hadley finished the third Peary sledge on the eleventh. On the same day I had the Eskimo build a large snow igloo on the floe where we had our box-house of supplies, to furnish additional shelter for ourselves and the dogs. We began making wooden boxes for the protection of our Primus stoves in case we had to take to the ice. The Primus stove is an ingenious device for heating tea or whatever else you have that needs heating; it uses kerosene oil, ignited by means of alcohol, works somewhat like a plumber's torch and has long been used by men engaged in Arctic work. It is not so efficient as the special alcohol stove invented by Peary for his expeditions but as a general rule it does good work. On our trip to Wrangell Island, we used gasoline in these stoves, although warned by the directions in big red letters not to do so. In spite of the directions the gasoline worked well and did not need to be ignited by alcohol.

On the sixteenth I had the Eskimo dig out the seal meat which we had kept in the "ice-houses" near the ship and put it on deck, so that we could have it handy in case the ice broke up around the ship. Furthermore, I wanted to see how much we had accumulated. I found that we had forty-one seal, about 1600 pounds, enough to last twenty-five people sixty-seven days. Not every one on board liked seal meat but all could eat it. I had Mamen at work these days making up a list of things required in case I went on another Arctic drift some time. Murray lost his dredge again on the eighteenth when it caught on the ice and parted the line; the chief engineer started work at once on another.

December 21 was the Arctic midnight, the day of days in the Arctic, the day that we all looked forward to, for now the sun was coming towards us every day, and every day the daylight would lengthen. We were not, of course, getting real daylight but at midday we got a kind of twilight that was good enough to get about by, out of doors. Mr. Hadley and I experimented with the acetylene lights but found that outside of the ship they would not work because the water froze.

On the twenty-second much of the twilight time was used in clearing away the huge banks of snow that had drifted about the ship. The chess tournament was decided on that day. The men had been playing it for a good while and now the winner of the most games received the first prize, a box of fifty cigars, and the next man the second prize, a box of twenty-five cigars. Mamen took the first prize and the mate, Mr. Anderson, the second.

The dogs, which we had been keeping all together

in the box-house, broke their chains on the twenty-
third, and some of them got into a fight; our best
dog, Jack, was so badly bitten that he could not
walk. I took him on board and down into the carpenter's shop where Mr. Hadley sewed up his
wounds with surgical needle and silk cord. Poor
Jack was in bad shape and at first refused all food.
He received constant attention from Mr. Hadley
out could not bear a harness until the latter part of
February. The fight in which he was hurt warned
us that we must not keep too many dogs together,
so I had the Eskimo build several snow kennels in a large snowbank near the ship. They
sprinkled ashes on the floor of the kennels and
chained up the nine most quarrelsome dogs, each
in his separate kennel.

With the approach of Christmas all hands began
to make plans for the proper celebration of that
good old holiday. The spirits of the whole party
were excellent; now that they were in the neighborhood of the place where Santa Claus came from
they seemed determined to observe the day in a
manner worthy of the jolly old saint.

At six o'clock on Christmas morning the second
engineer and McKinlay started in decorating the
cabin with the flags of the International Code and
a fine lot of colored ribbon which Mr. Hadley had
brought with him from Point Barrow for the trad-

ing he had hoped to do in Banks Land. Later in the morning I went around and distributed presents to the Eskimo. I gave each of the Eskimo men a hunting-knife and a watch and the Eskimo woman a cotton dress, stockings and underwear, talcum powder, soap, a looking-glass, a comb and brush and some ribbon, with a cotton dress for each of the little girls.

At eleven o'clock the first event on our typewritten programme began—the sports. This was the list:

D. G. S. *Karluk*. XMAS DAY, 1913

The events of the sports programme arranged for the day will take place in the following order:

1. 100 yards sprint
2. Long jump (standing)
3. Long jump (running)
4. Sack race
5. High jump
    Interval for refreshments
6. Three-legged race
7. Putting the weight
8. 50-yard burst
9. Hop, step and leap
10. Tug of war
11. Obstacle race
12. Wrestling

Proceedings will commence at 11 A. M. (*Karluk* time); dogs and bookmakers not allowed on the field.

The doctor was umpire and wore a paper rosette.

I was the official starter and fired a pistol in the regulation manner.

Mamen won the running long jump and would have won all the other jumps and races if he had entered them. The obstacle race was funny to watch and greatly enjoyed. The contestants started on the ice on the starboard side about amidships. From here they had to go to, and under, the jib-boom from which hung loops of rope; they had to pass through these loops and then under some sledges turned bottom up. Then they had to keep on around the ship to a kind of track which we had dug in a snowbank running at right angles to the ship; the track was just wide enough for a man to put both feet in and they had to go up the track and down again. This was no easy task and it was a cause for hilarious mirth to watch them trying to pass each other in the narrow path. Then they had to go to the dredge igloo where life-belts had been placed, each marked with its owner's name. Each man had to find his own life-belt and put it on just as he would wear it if he were called upon to use it. It was pitch dark in the igloo; a man would rush in, pick up a life-belt and rush out again on to the ice to look at the belt in the twilight and see if it were his. It often took a man several trips to find his own. Then they made the final dash to the starting-point and the first man home with his life-belt on, as if for regular use, won the race. Williamson, the second engineer, was the winner.

The Eskimo entered all the sports and even Keruk took part in most of them. I pulled in the tug of war, to make both sides even, and I am proud to say that my side won. We did not have the wrestling-match because it got too dark to see.

It was a fine day and the men wore American clothes and sweaters. For several days before Christmas we had had a severe storm with a high wind which blew the tops of the ice ridges bare of snow and gave the scene the appearance of a ploughed field. On Christmas Eve, however, the wind subsided so that all day long on Christmas Day we had good weather, clear, crisp air, with a temperature of twenty below zero.

Dinner as usual was at half past four. I confess that I felt homesick and thought of other Christmas dinners. It was my fourth Christmas in the Arctic; in 1898 I had been with Peary at Cape D'Urville on the *Windward* and in 1905 and 1908 at Cape Sheridan with the *Roosevelt,* but our situation now had far more elements of uncertainty in it than we had felt on those occasions and in addition this time it was I who had the responsibility for the lives and fortunes of every man, woman and child in the party.

We sat down at 4:30 P. M. to a menu laid out and typewritten by McKinlay:

"Such a bustle ensued"

Mixed Pickles   Sweet Pickles
Oyster Soup
Lobster
Bear Steak
Ox Tongue

Potatoes   Green Peas
Asparagus and Cream Sauce
Mince Pie   Plum Pudding
Mixed Nuts
Tea   Cake
Strawberries

"God Bless You, Merry Gentlemen;
May Nothing You Dismay!"

Murray produced a cake which had been given in Victoria to cut for this particular occasion and which he had kept carefully secreted. Dinner, which was a great credit to Bob, the cook, was followed by cigars and cigarettes and a concert on the Victrola which had been presented to the ship by Sir Richard McBride. We had records that played both classical and popular music, vocal and instrumental, and we kept this up with singing, to a late hour. Malloch wrote a Christmas letter of many pages to his father, a letter which, alas, was destined never to be delivered.

On Friday the twenty-sixth a crack in the ice made from the waist of the ship towards the stern,

running for about a hundred yards off the starboard
bow. The crack did not open, but for the first
time in our drift we felt a slight tremor on the ship.
In about an hour we felt another slight tremor. I
followed the crack for a hundred yards and then
lost it. There was a fresh north-northeast wind
which moderated as the day wore on but it looked
as if we were in for some more bad weather, though
the barometer was steady, and next day we began to
get things ready to leave the ship at once, in case
we should have to get out in a hurry. Everything
was where we could lay our hands on it at
once.

Our soundings had been giving us depths of
about twenty-five fathoms, which did not tally with
our charts. It seemed likely that our chronometer
was a trifle slow and that we were somewhat to the
westward of our apparent position. We had a
clear view of the sky with a very pronounced twilight glow to the south.

On the twenty-eighth we altered the ship's time
again to get the benefit of the increasing twilight.
Molly gave birth to a litter of nine pups, which, if
she had not eaten most of them, would have been
useful members of the party, had our drift continued for another year so that they could have
grown large enough to use. The prizes won on
Christmas Day were now distributed: safety razors

and extra blades, shaving-soap, hair-clippers, goggles, pipes, sweaters, shirts, and various other things.

As soon as it was light on the twenty-ninth I kept a sharp eye out for land; south by west, by the compass, I could see a blue cloud raised up on the horizon. According to the soundings we should have been nearer Wrangell Island than Herald Island; I was inclined to think that it was Herald Island, although working out our position with our chronometer readings gave us Herald Island sixty miles to the south. Afterwards I found out that our observations at this time were correct but that the soundings were not right on the chart. What deceived us more than anything else was the big mirage; Herald Island looked large and distorted for many days. Later in the day I went aloft to see if I could make out which island it really was but on account of the imperfect light I found it impossible to tell.

Some time during the night the ice cracked about a hundred yards from the ship and made an open ribbon of water ten inches wide; during the next day the young ice was cracking a good deal all around us. There was no lateral movement of the ice.

The next day was the last day of 1913. Our time was six hours and thirty-six minutes later than

Boston and New York time and as the day wore on and it got to be 5:24 P. M. I realized that it was midnight on Tremont Street and Broadway and I thought of the friends who would now be seeing the old year out and the new year in. I wondered what they thought had become of us on the *Karluk,* and whether the news of our unforeseen drift had yet reached them from Stefansson. I could picture the carefree throngs in the hotels waiting for the lights to go out for the moment of midnight and greeting 1914 with a cheer and a song.

We had our own New Year's celebration, though it was only a coincidence that it came on this particular day, for we had planned a football game on the ice when the weather should be good and the wind fairly light; New Year's Day happened to be the first good day for it.

The ball was made of seal-gut, cut into sections and sewed up, with surgeon's plaster over the seams. We blew it up with a pipe stem and plugged up the hole. To protect the ball we had a sealskin casing made to fit it; the result was a fairly good ball, constructed on the same principle as any college football.

It was Scotland vs. All-Nations; the game was association football, played on a field of regulation size laid out on young ice about a foot and a half in thickness. At each end of the field were goal posts with the usual cross-bar.

Fireman Breddy was captain of All-Nations and Mr. Munro of Scotland. The Eskimo, though not well-versed in the game, played well. Keruk, clad as usual in dress and bloomers, was goal-tender for All-Nations. Some of the players wore skin-boots, others ordinary American shoes. I had forgotten a good deal about the association game but I refreshed my memory from the encyclopedia in the ship's library and armed with a mouth-organ in lieu of a whistle took my place as referee, umpire and time-keeper. I soon found, however, that the cold would make it too dangerous for me to use the "whistle," for it would freeze to my lips and take the skin off, so I had to give my signals for play by word of mouth.

The teams lined up at 11:30. Breddy won the toss and took the western end of the field. All-Nations scored the first goal and the play ranged furiously up and down the field until the first thirty-minute period was over. Then at noon we had an intermission and served coffee. At half-past twelve the teams lined up again, with changed goals. During the second half Scotland played well but when the game ended the score stood: All-Nations, 8; Scotland, 3. Another game was planned for the following Sunday.

CHAPTER XI

THE SINKING OF THE *KARLUK*

During the night of New Year's Day we could hear, when we were below, a rumbling noise not unlike that which one often hears singing along the telegraph wires on a country road. The sound was inaudible from the deck. It was clear that there was tremendous pressure somewhere, though there were no visible indications of it in the vicinity of the ship. We were practically stationary. Apparently the great field of ice in which we had been zigzagging for so many months had finally brought up on the shore of Wrangell Island and was comparatively at rest, while the running ice outside this great field was still in active motion and tended to force the ice constantly in the direction of the island.

On Saturday, with a fresh north wind, in spite of which ship and ice still remained stationary, the rumbling noise could again be heard in the interior of the ship.

On Sunday the fourth there was an increasing easterly wind which sent us slowly westward. Evidently we could make no movement towards the

south on account of the pressure but when the wind
blew us towards the west and north we could
go along without undue danger. The football
game was played as planned on this day until
the second engineer strained a muscle in his leg
kicking the ball along the ice, and the game had
to stop.

The easterly gale continued for several days,
sometimes with hard snowstorms, sometimes with
clearer skies. The barometer was low; the temperature rose to sixteen degrees above zero. I had
the engineers at work making tins of one-gallon
capacity to hold kerosene for our sledges if we
should have to use them. All of our oil was in five-
gallon tins which were unhandy for sledging use.
They also made tea-boilers out of gasoline tins, to be
used with the Primus stoves; these held about a gallon of tea and were very handy. I had five with me
on my subsequent sledge trip. Besides these jobs
the engineers trimmed down our pickaxes so that
they would weigh not over two-and-a-half or three
pounds. They put them in the portable forge in
the engine-room, heated the iron and beat it down,
and put on the steel tips afterwards. These pickaxes were regulation miners' picks.

On the seventh and eighth the variable weather
continued with occasional twilight of considerable
intensity; the low barometer and high thermometer

still prevailed. Our observations on the seventh, the last we were to take on shipboard, gave us our position as Lat. 72.11 N., Long. 174.36 W. The temperature dropped on the ninth; the sky, which was clear in the morning, became overcast by afternoon and the wind shifted from southeast to southwest. We were getting nearer the land and the ice was raftering in places with the pressure, so that I felt sure that something was going to happen before long. We continued our preparations for putting emergency supplies in condition to be handled quickly, putting tea tablets in tins made by the engineers, and twenty-two calibre cartridges in similar tins. Mannlicher cartridges we put up in packages of thin canvas, fifty to a package.

At five o'clock on the morning of the tenth I was awakened by a loud report like a rifle-shot. Then there came a tremor all through the ship. I was soon on deck. The watchman, who for that night was Brady, had already been overboard on the ice and I met him coming up the ice gangway to tell me what he had found. There was a small crack right at the stem of the ship, he said. I went there with him at once and found that the crack ran irregularly but in general northwesterly for about two hundred yards. At first it was very slight, although it was a clean and unmistakable break; in the course of half an hour, however, it grew to a foot in width and as the day wore on widened still more until it was two feet wide on an average.

By 10 A. M. there was a narrow lane of water off both bow and stern. The ship was now entirely free on the starboard side but still frozen fast in her ice-cradle on the port side; her head was pointed southwest. On account of the way in which the ice had split the ship was held in a kind of pocket; the wind, which was light and from the north in the earlier part of the day, hauled to the northwest towards afternoon and increased to a gale, with blinding snowdrift, and the sheet of ice on the starboard side began to move astern, only a little at a time. The ship felt no pressure, only slight shocks, and her hull was still untouched, for the open ends of the pocket fended off the moving ice, especially at the stern. It was clear to me, however, that as soon as the moving ice should grind or break off the points of these natural fenders there was a strong probability that the moving ice-sheet would draw nearer to the starboard side of the ship and, not unlike the jaws of a nut-cracker, squeeze her against the sheet in which she was frozen on the port side, particularly as the wind was attaining a velocity of forty-five miles an hour.

Everything indicated, therefore, that the time

was near at hand when we should have to leave the ship. We must have things ready. I gave orders to get the snow off the deck and the skylights and the outer walls of the cabin, to lighten her. Some of the men were sent over to the box-house to remove the few dogs that were still tethered there and set them free on the ice, and to get the house ready in case we had to move into it. They cleaned it up, put fresh boards on the floor and laid a fire in the stove, ready for lighting.

The men worked with good spirit and seemed unperturbed. I sent them about their daily tasks, as usual, so far as possible, and the preparation of the box-house was in the nature of an emergency drill. For if the points of the ice should continue unbroken the ship would still be saved; we had seen plenty of cracks before in our drift that had remained open some time and then closed up again, though of course no previous break had come so near the ship. It was hard to see what was going on around us for the sky was overcast and the darkness was the kind which, as the time-honored phrase goes, you could cut with a knife, while the stinging snowdrift, whirling and eddying through the air, under the impetus of the screaming gale, added to the uncertainty as to what was about to happen from moment to moment.

At about half past seven in the evening I

chanced to be standing near the engine-room door. The lamps were lighted. The labors of the day were over and now, after dinner, the men were playing cards or reading or sewing, as usual. All at once I heard a splitting, crashing sound below. I went down into the engine-room and found the chief engineer there. We could hear water rushing into the hold and by lantern-light could see it pouring in at different places for a distance of ten feet along the port side. As I had feared, the ice astern had broken or worn off and the sheet moving along the starboard side had swung in against the ship, heeling her over three or four feet to port; a point of ice on the port side had pierced the planking and timbers of the engine-room for ten feet or more, ripping off all the pump fixtures and putting the pump out of commission. It was obvious that it would be useless to attempt to rig a temporary pump; the break was beyond repair.

I went on deck again and gave the order, " All hands abandon ship." We had all the fires except that in the galley extinguished at once and all the lamps, using hurricane lanterns to see our way around. There was no confusion. The men worked with a will, putting the emergency supplies overboard on the ice, some ten thousand pounds of pemmican, furs, clothing, rifles and cartridges. The Eskimo woman, with her children, I sent to the box-house to start the fire in the stove and keep the place warm. The steward was kept in the galley so that the men could have coffee and hot food.

By 10.45 P. M. there was eleven feet of water in the engine-room. At this stage the pressure of the ice on both sides kept the ship from going down. We were less than an hour getting the supplies off the ship on to the ice; we could have saved every-thing on board but no attempt was made to save luxuries or souvenirs or personal belongings above the essentials, for it did not seem advisable to bur-den the sledges on our prospective journey over the ice with loads of material that would have to occupy space needed for indispensables.

When I was satisfied with the amount of sup-plies on the ice I started the men sledging the stuff over to the big floe. Here, as I have said, in addi-tion to the box-house, we had a large snow igloo which had been completed some time before. It had been smashed in by the wind, but the men now repaired it and made it ready for occupancy. They did a good job with their evening's work and I told them so, and said that they could turn in at the box-house and igloo and go to sleep whenever they got their sledging done. At half-past two in the morning they were ready and turned in; to the box-house were assigned McKinlay, Mamen, Beuchat,

Murray, Dr. Mackay, Williams, King, Chafe, Kataktovick and Kerdrillo and his family, and to the snow igloo Munro, Williamson, Breddy, Hadley, Templeman, Maurer, Brady, Anderson, Barker, Malloch and myself.

After every one else had left the ship I remained on board to await the end. For a time the chief engineer and Hadley stayed with me. There was a big fire in the galley and we moved the Victrola in there to while away the time. After the first sharp crash and the closing in of the ice the pressure was not heavy and all through the morning of the eleventh and well into the afternoon, the ship remained in about the same position as when she was first struck. No more water was coming in; the ice was holding her up. I would play a few records—we had a hundred and fifty or so altogether—and then I would go outside and walk around the deck, watching for any change in the ship's position. It cleared off towards noon and there was a little twilight but the snow was still blowing. As I played the records I threw them into the stove. At last I found Chopin's *Funeral March,* played it over and laid it aside. I ate when I was hungry and had plenty of coffee and tea. My companions had gone over to the floe and turned in early in the morning. It was quite comfortable in the galley, for I could keep the fire going with coal from the galley locker. At times I would take a look into the engine-room, being careful not to get too far from an exit; the water was nearly up to the deck.

At 3.15 P.M. the ice opened and the ship began to get lower in the water. Then the ice closed up again for a while and supported her by the bowsprit and both quarters. About half past three she began to settle in earnest and as the minutes went by the decks were nearly a-wash. Putting Chopin's *Funeral March* on the Victrola, I started the machine and when the water came running along the deck and poured down the hatches, I stood up on the rail and as she took a header with the rail level with the ice I stepped off. It was at 4 P. M. on January 11, 1914, with the blue Canadian Government ensign at her main-topmast-head, blowing out straight and cutting the water as it disappeared, and the Victrola in the galley sending out the strains of Chopin's *Funeral March,* that the *Karluk* sank, going down by the head in thirty-eight fathoms of water. As she took the final plunge, I bared my head and said, *"Adios, Karluk!"* It was light enough to see and the rest of the party came out of the camp to watch the end. As she went down the yards lodged on the ice and broke off; in such a narrow lane of water did she disappear.

It is always a tragic moment when a ship sinks, the ship that has been your home for months; it is not unlike losing some good and faithful friend. Twice before I had been shipwrecked, on both occasions on the southern coast of Newfoundland, so the sensation was not altogether new to me, but it was none the less poignant. Yet I could feel no despair in our present situation, for we had comfortable quarters on a floe which was practically indestructible and plenty of food and fuel, so that with patience, perseverance, courage and good fortune we should be able to win our way back to safety in due time.

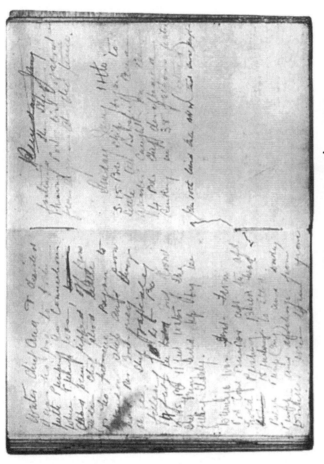

PAGES FROM CAPTAIN BARTLETT'S DIARY

"Sunday, Jan'y 11th. 3.15 p. m. ship began to settle till bowsprit and quarter caught on ice. 4 p. m. ship disappeared sinking in 38 fathoms water."

CHAPTER XII

The point where the *Karluk* went down was hard by the place where the *Jeannette* of the De Long expedition was frozen in the ice and began her westward drift to a point off Henrietta Island, where she was crushed, in much the same manner as the *Karluk*, by the opening and closing of the ice, and sank June 12, 1881. As I study the map of the polar regions and see how we drifted from a point near the 145th meridian to a point near the 175th meridian, west longitude, and how the *Jeannette* drifted from a point near the 175th meridian, west longitude, to a point near the 155th meridian, east longitude, and then how the *Fram* drifted from a point near the 140th meridian, east longitude, to a point near the 10th meridian, east longitude, and realize that the sum of these three drifts embraces more than half the distance around the continental periphery, I can not help coming to the conclusion that the idea of casks and wreckage drifting across the Pole from the waters of Alaska and Siberia to the Greenland Sea opposite is a mistaken one. Wreckage from the *Jeannette* drifted ashore on the southern coast of Greenland in 1884, and this gave Dr. Nansen the idea on which he based his expedition in the *Fram,* that a ship allowed to freeze in the ice north of the New Siberian Islands, near the point where the *Jeannette* sank, would be carried by the currents in a drift across the Pole. Nansen himself left the *Fram* in the course of her drift and made a journey over the ice in an attempt to reach the Pole, getting to 86° 34 N., and after his departure the *Fram,* in her drift, reached almost as high a latitude as he attained on foot, without, however, giving evidence of the accuracy of the theory of a drift across the Pole. I believe, that the drift follows the general outline of the land, from east to west around the periphery of the Arctic Ocean, and that a craft, built in general like the *Roosevelt* but not so large, with a ship's company of eight who should be crew and scientific staff in one, could follow this drift from beginning to end, and would, in a period of three or four years, cover the greater part of the circuit of the Arctic Ocean.

Such an expedition would add much to our scientific knowledge of the Arctic regions, working out the ocean currents, exploring the floor of the sea, obtaining accurate soundings for plotting positions on the chart, outlining the continental shelf, gathering information about the air currents for the use of students of aviation, collecting valuable meteorological data, continuous for the period of the drift, for the use of weather bureaus, and perhaps making possible the finding of new lands in the vast unexplored region north of Siberia. England and Norway have turned their attention to the Antarctic and it is America's place to undertake the task of completing our knowledge of the Arctic, so far advanced through centuries of Anglo-Saxon endeavor. As Nansen said, in stating his plans for his expedition in the *Fram:* "People, perhaps, still exist who believe that it is of no importance to explore the unknown polar regions. This, of course, shows ignorance. It is hardly necessary to mention here of what scientific importance it is that these regions should be thoroughly explored. The history of the human race is a continual struggle from darkness towards light. It is, therefore, to no purpose to discuss the use of knowledge; man wants to know, and when he ceases to do so, he is no longer man."

As soon as the *Karluk* sank, I turned in at the igloo to have a good sleep, for I had been awake since five o'clock on the morning of the tenth, and it was now late in the afternoon of the eleventh.

It was nearly noon of the next day before I awoke. The sky was clear overhead but the fresh northwest wind kept the snow spinning over the ice and there was still only a brief twilight in the middle of the day. As soon as they could see their way around in this half light, I had all hands at work picking up the odds and ends scattered about on the ice and had a tent erected to house the supplies sledged from the ship on the previous night.

In this tent, into which no one was allowed to go but McKinlay, who acted as a kind of stock-clerk, and myself, were placed the following supplies which will show how well equipped we were with the essentials for life in the Arctic:

     70 suits Jaeger underwear
      6 sweaters
      3 dozen wool shirts
    200 pairs stockings
      3 bolts of gaberdine
      6 fleece suits
      4 Burberry hunting suits
      2 large sacks of deer legs
      2 large sacks of waterskin boots (sealskin
          boots for shedding water)
    100 pairs of mukluks
    100 fawn skins
      1 dozen hair-seal skins
      2 ugsug skins
     20 reindeer skins
      6 large winter reindeer skins
     50 Jaeger blankets
     20 mattresses

On the floe itself and arranged to be easily accessible were:

4056 pounds of Underwood pemmican
5222 pounds of Hudson's Bay pemmican
   3 drums of coal oil
  15 cases of coal oil
   2 boxes of tea
 200 tins of milk
 250 pounds of sugar
   2 boxes of chocolate
   2 boxes of butter
   1 box of cocoa
Candles and matches

Besides these supplies in the tent and on the floe we had, of course, the coal, clothing, and equipment which we had been placing on the ice through the previous months, consisting, besides ammunition, pemmican, milk, clothing, tea, coffee, sugar, and butter, of these things:

 250 sacks of coal
  33 cases of gasoline
   1 case of codfish
   3 large cases of cod steak
   5 drums of alcohol
   4 cases of desiccated eggs
 114 cases of pilot bread, each case containing 48 pounds in small tins
   5 barrels of beef
   9 sledges, each capable of carrying 600 or 700 pounds
2000 feet of lumber
   3 coal stoves
   2 wood stoves
  90 feet of stove-pipe
   1 extra suit of sails
   2 Peterborough canoes

The snow igloo was fifteen feet long and twelve feet wide, with rafters and a canvas roof. The box-house was twenty-five feet long by eighteen feet wide, well banked up all around with snow. We partitioned off one end of the box-house to make the galley and put a big stove in it so that the cook could have a place by himself. We also built another house for the Eskimo. McKinlay afterwards drew a plan of Shipwreck Camp, as we called it, which will show how our dwelling-places and supplies were arranged.

So here we were, like the Swiss Family Robinson, well equipped for comfortable living, waiting until the return of the sun should give us daylight enough for ice travel, which was altogether too exacting and dangerous to attempt in the dark. I did not consider it wise to use up the energy of men and dogs when they were still unaccustomed to travelling over the sea-ice and before there was light enough to make their work effective.

The place where the ship had gone down was frozen over. The ice had simply opened for a while and then closed up again, and young ice had formed in the opening.

On the thirteenth we began sewing and kept it up day in and day out. We had done a good deal of sewing on shipboard, but I told the men that we must have plenty of fur clothing and skin-boots and

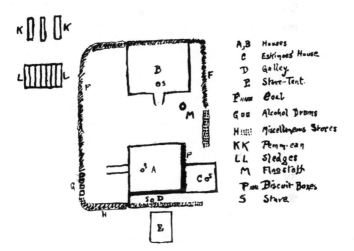

PLAN OF SHIPWRECK CAMP

10TH JANUARY TO
1914.

A,B Houses
C   Eskimoes' House
D   Galley.
E   Store-Tent.
P   Coal
G   Alcohol Drums
H   Miscellaneous Stores
KK   Pemmican
LL   Sledges
M   Flagstaff
P   Biscuit Boxes
S   Stove

that we had better do all the sewing we could.   We also made tents and covers of light canvas for our sledges.   We should of course be unable to do any sewing when we once got under way for the land. We had lanterns and lamps for light in the various houses.

Fur clothing is so heavy that it has to be sewed by hand but much of the other work was done on sewing-machines of which we had saved two, one for the box-house and the other for the snow igloo. Keruk used one sewing-machine and Mr. Munro the other.   He was skilful at this as at a good many other useful things.   He had formerly been a junior officer on the British warship *Rainbow,* which was afterwards transferred to the Canadian service; his term of enlistment expired at the time of the transfer and Captain Hose of the *Rainbow,* commandant of the Esquimault Navy Yard, recommended him to me for chief engineer of the *Karluk.*

On the fourteenth it was fine and clear with a temperature of thirty-eight degrees below zero. The wind was west; our soundings through a hole cut in the ice gave us thirty-four fathoms.   In the noon twilight we could see land in a southwesterly direction.   The men worked all day long making footbags to use when sleeping; it would be a great relief to take off the deerskin boots and put on these footbags, which had fur inside and Burberry cloth outside. I had with me a coonskin coat which I had bought a few years before in Boston. I now cut this up and divided it among the men, as far as it would go, to be made into these footbags. In addition I told each man that he must have at least four pair of deerskin or sheepskin stockings and three pair of deerskin boots. We used scissors and knives to cut the skins into suitable pieces for making boots and clothing. The Eskimos used a crescent-shaped implement called the *hudlow,* not unlike a mince-meat chopper; they could use it very deftly and cut out clothing exceedingly well with it. The skins had to be softened, as I have mentioned before, by breaking the vellum; this was done by scraping it with a piece of iron like a chisel. Some Eskimo women soften the vellum by chewing it.

We conducted our lives according to a regular routine similar to that which we had followed on shipboard during the last few months of our drift. We kept our records of wind and weather, of soundings and of temperature, which remained in the minus thirties for a good many days. We did not bother with latitude as we had the land in view some sixty to eighty miles away, not distinctly visible but plain enough on a clear day when the light was fairly good. The light of course came from the south and the land, being in that direction, was set off by the twilight glow, and the sun was getting nearer and nearer to the horizon as the days went by. We saved a chronometer from the ship but it got somewhat banged about in the transfer from the ship to the camp, so that we could not depend upon it. I had a watch which I have carried for a number of years and which I was careful never to allow to run down.

Each house had a watchman, every man taking his turn. It was his duty to keep the fires going. At 6 A. M. the watchman would call the cook; our meal hours were the same as those which we had observed during the past few months on the ship.

Lights were out at 10 P. M. and all hands turned in. We had a stove in the centre of the room in each house and around the stove on three sides, built out from the walls, were the bed-platforms, which came close to the stove and were on a somewhat higher level. Here we slept warmly and comfortably on the mattresses we had saved from the ship.

There was plenty to occupy our minds. In addition to our sewing and other daily tasks, there was time for games of chess and cards and frequently of an evening we would gather around the fire and have a "sing." Sometimes, too, we would dance; I remember one night catching hold of

some one and taking a turn or two on the floor
when we tipped over the stove.   It took some lively
work to get it set up again.

The *Karluk* had a good library and we saved a
number of books which enabled some of us to catch
up a little on our reading.   We read such books as
"Wuthering Heights," "Villette," and "Jane
Eyre," besides more recent novels.   My own constant companion, which I have never tired of reading, was the "Rubaiyat" of Omar Khayyam.   I
have a leather-bound copy of this which was given
me by Charles Arthur Moore, Jr., who, with Harry
Whitney and a number of other Yale friends of
his, was with me on a hunting trip in Hudson's
Bay on the sealer *Algerine* in 1901.   This book I
have carried with me everywhere since then, until
now, if it had not been repaired in various places
by surgeon's plaster, I believe it would fall to
pieces.   I have had it with me on voyages to South
America and other foreign parts on sailing vessels
when I was serving my years of apprenticeship to
get my British master's certificate in 1905; on both
of my trips with Peary as captain of the *Roosevelt;*
on my trip to Europe with Peary after the attainment of the North Pole; on a hunting trip in the
Arctic on the *Boeothic* in the summer of 1910,
when we brought home the musk-oxen and the polar
bear, Silver King, to the Bronx Park Zoo in New

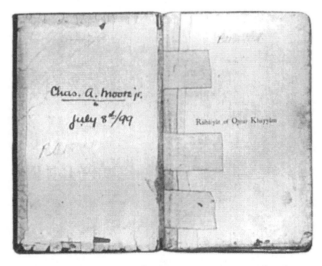

CAPTAIN BARTLETT'S COPY OF THE RUBÁIYÁT OF OMAR KHAYYAM

" My own constant companion, which I have never tired of reading, was the ' Rubáiyát ' of Omar Khayyam. This book I have carried with me everywhere."

York; on various sealing trips; and now the self-same copy was with me on the *Karluk* and afterwards on my journey to bring about the rescue of our ship's company. I have read it over and over again and never seem to tire of it. Perhaps it is because there is something in its philosophy which appeals to my own feeling about life and death. For all my experience and observation leads me to the conclusion that we are to die at the time appointed and not before; this is, I suppose, what is known as fatalism.

On the night of the fourteenth the dogs had a fight and one of them was killed. We could ill afford to lose him, for dogs were at a premium with us, now.

On the fifteenth, sixteenth and seventeenth the weather was threatening; the sky was overcast and the wind from the north and northeast, with temperatures not far from forty below zero. The sewing continued busily. On the sixteenth we overhauled our Primus stoves, of which we had two of the Swedish and eight of the Lovett pattern. We also reckoned the amount of oil necessary for them and found that an imperial gallon, which would fill a stove three and a half times, would make tea twice a day for fourteen days. The imperial or English gallon is larger than the American gallon; ten gallons English would mean a little

CHAPTER XIII

On January seventeenth I decided that before long I would send a party of four men to the land to look out for game, see whether any driftwood was to be found on Wrangell Island, report on ice conditions and blaze a trail over the ice. This expedition would make an end to the men's enforced inactivity and the natural uneasiness of some of them, which I was unwilling to prolong if I could avoid doing so, and would, besides, be valuable in determining our subsequent movements. I did not like to take the whole party to the island without previously transporting supplies that would be sure to last them for at least four months. Furthermore, the men had been living for a long time on shipboard and were not inured to the cold or yet in condition to withstand the privations they would have to undergo. None of them had had any experience in travelling over the Arctic ice during the brief and meagre light and in the low temperatures which would be our portion for another month, and the sledging of supplies towards the island would afford them the necessary practice.

Travelling over the sea-ice at any time is altogether
different from land travelling. On the sea-ice you
have to spend a great deal of time looking about for
good places to make the road for the sledging of
supplies, for the ice is continually cracking and
shifting and piling up in fantastic ridges from the
pressure when the fissures close up, especially as
near the land as we were, and its surface is so much
rougher than the crystal levels of the lakes and
ponds on which the landsman goes skating that
there can hardly be said to be any comparison.

For the past week or so, I had noticed that our
drift was slow, and I felt that as the daylight
lengthened we should have ample time, long before
we could drift away from the land, to sledge
enough supplies ashore to last the party until the
birds returned and the ice broke up. If we could
start the men in small parties to relay supplies to
the island we could get a shore camp established
where the men could dry out their foot-gear for
their journey back over the ice to Shipwreck Camp
for more supplies, especially if we should find
plenty of driftwood on Wrangell Island, as I
hoped and expected; we had fuel enough at the
camp to last a year. The men could erect permanent snow igloos along the way, for relay stations,
and once the road to the island was made, there
would be little difficulty in keeping it open and by

THE ICE-PACK

"On the sea-ice you have to spend a great deal of time looking about for good places to make the road for the sledging of supplies, for the ice is continually cracking and shifting and piling up."

continuing the relays any faults that might come in the trail could be easily repaired. In these preliminary journeys, as I have said, the men would get accustomed to ice travel and finally the whole party, with its supplies, would be safe ashore. We were of course handicapped by lack of sufficient dogs, and in ice travel and in fact in any polar work, dogs are the prime requisites for success; man-power for hauling the sledge-loads of supplies puts a double burden on the men.

Those assigned for the first shoregoing party were First Mate Anderson, Second Mate Barker and Sailors King and Brady. They were to go to the island with three sledges and eighteen dogs, with Mamen and the two Eskimo men, as a supporting party, to come back with the dogs and two of the sledges after they had landed the mate's party on the island.

The eighteenth was another bad day, with a strong northeast gale and blinding snowdrift. Some of the men were at work loading the three sledges for the mate's party. Of the others, those that could be spared I sent out with pickaxes to make a trail towards the land, so that the shoregoing party might have a good start, but the weather was so bad that they had to return to camp after they had gone two or three miles. They reported seeing bear tracks on the ice and seal in open

leads which they came to. We had plenty of seal
meat so no attempt was made to do any shooting at
this time.

Mr. Anderson, McKinlay and myself checked
over the three sledge-loads on the nineteenth and
found everything in readiness for the journey
which was to begin the next morning. The next
day, however, the bad weather continued. The
watchman called me at 4 A. M. and I found a southwest gale blowing, with a thick snowstorm, so, as
there was no change in the weather, the mate's
party did not leave. In the afternoon the storm
subsided and by midnight the sky was clear and the
air calm and cold.

The next day, Wednesday the twenty-first, conditions were more favorable and the party started.
In addition to oral instructions about ice conditions and about returning to camp in case he met
with open water, I gave the mate the following
written orders:

> SHIPWRECK CAMP, ARCTIC OCEAN,
>   January 20, 1914.
>
> *My dear Mr. Anderson:*
>   You will leave to-morrow morning with Mamen,
> three sledges, 18 dogs, Mr. Barker, Sailors King
> and Brady and the two Eskimo. The sledges are
> loaded with pemmican, biscuit and oil. You will
> find list of articles attached to this. When you
> reach Berry Point, Wrangell Island, you will be

in charge of supplies. Kindly pay special attention to the uses of them. The rations are: 1 lb.
pemmican, 1 lb. biscuits, with tea, per day. One
gallon of oil will last you ten days. Mamen will
leave one sledge and the tent, taking back with him
enough supplies to carry him to Shipwreck.
Whilst on the island you will endeavor to find
game. Be sure and bring it to your camp. Also
collect all the driftwood you can find.

Very sincerely,
R. A. BARTLETT.

The list of things carried on the sledge may
serve to show what the Arctic traveller needs.
Shelter, fuel and food, these are the three essentials
for ice travel as they are for the journey of life
itself. This is the way the mate's party was
equipped when it set out from Shipwreck Camp on
January 21, 1914; there were enough supplies to
last them for three months:

FIRST SLEDGE:

4 cases of man pemmican
1 tin of Hudson's Bay pemmican
10 gallons of coal oil
2400 tea tablets
1 tent and fly
1 Primus stove
46 lbs. of biscuits
500 22-cartridges
1 22-rifle
Candles, matches, pickaxes
1 sledge cover

SECOND SLEDGE:

  25 lbs. of sugar
   4 cases of dog pemmican
   7 tins of Hudson's Bay pemmican
   2 cases of biscuits
   1 dozen milk
   1 Primus stove
   1 30–30 Winchester rifle
 100 30–30 cartridges
Candles, matches, pickaxe, hatchets
   1 sledge cover

THIRD SLEDGE:

   4 cases of dog pemmican
   2 cases of man pemmican
   7 tins of Hudson's Bay pemmican
   1 Mannlicher rifle
 250 Mannlicher cartridges
   1 one-gallon tin of coal oil
   2 bottles of alcohol
Pickaxe, hatchets, shovels, rope
Sleeping-robes and personal outfit
   1 pair of ski
   1 pair of snowshoes
   1 sledge cover

To Mamen I gave a brief letter of instructions, concluding with this paragraph: "Should you miss the trail and fail to connect with our camp, after a reasonable time has been spent in looking it up, you will go back to Wrangell Island and await my arriving there."

The party got away at 9.30 A. M., accompanied for about five miles by other members of the expedition to give them a good start. There was a strong east wind, with drifting snow, but the weather cleared later in the day and it grew calm in the evening. There was about four hours' light a day now good for travelling.

Beyond its representation on our charts, we knew little about Wrangell Island, the chief source of our information being a short section in the American "Coast Pilot," which read as follows: "This island was first seen by the exploring party under the Russian Admiral Wrangell and named after the leader, though he himself doubted its existence; its southwestern point lies due North (*true*) 109 miles from Cape North. It must have been known to the whalers, who, about the year 1849, commenced to visit this sea, and did so for many years in great numbers. The *Jeannette's* people also saw it for many days in their memorable drift northwestward; but the first person to land on it, of which we have any authentic information, was Lieut. Hooper of the U. S. S. *Corwin* in 1881, and later in the same year it was explored by parties from the U. S. S. *Rodgers,* these two vessels having been sent to search for or obtain information concerning the *Jeannette,* the remnant of whose crew were perishing in the delta of the Lena at the very time this island was being explored.

"Wrangell Island is about 75 miles long E. N.

W. and W. S. W., and from 25 to 30 miles wide,
not including the large bare sandspits which extend
a long way from the shore, as much as 12 miles in
one place from the northern side, and rather more
near the southwestern corner of the island. A
range of hills extends completely round the coast,
and a lower range traverses the centre of the island
from east to west, the whole island in fact being
a succession of hills, peaks and valleys. The
highest point appeared to be Berry peak, near the
centre of the island, about 2500 feet in height by
barometric measurement."

On the twenty-second I sent Chafe and Williams out to begin marking the landward trail with
empty pemmican tins. Pemmican has been the
staple article of food for polar expeditions for
many years and contains, in small compass, the
essentials adequate to support life. It is put up
by various packing-houses, expressly for such
needs as ours. I have lived for a hundred and
twenty days on pemmican, biscuit and tea and
found it amply sufficient. We had two kinds of
pemmican; one, for ourselves, consisting of beef,
raisins, sugar and suet, all cooked together and
pressed, was packed in blue tins; the other, for the
dogs, without the raisins and sugar, in red tins.

I remember once, after a talk which I was giving
on the North Pole trip, a lady came up to me and

inquired what pemmican was, which I had mentioned several times. I explained what it was made of and what it was used for. She thought for a moment and then said, "Well, what I don't understand is how you shoot them."

Pemmican tins hold six pounds, marked so that you can tell how to take out exactly a pound, which, with tea and a pound of biscuit, is the standard daily ration per man. These tins are about fourteen inches in length, five in width and three in thickness. We would open a tin on one side and use up the contents; then we would open out the other side and flatten them all down to make a sheet. Plastered against an ice pinnacle to mark the trail or indicate a fault or the proximity of open water, these red or blue sheets of tin were visible against their white background for a mile and a half or two miles. This was one of the many things which I learned on my expeditions with Peary. Mamen had instructions to blaze his trail in this way so that he could find his way back. Marking the trail from the camp landward would now give the men training in ice travel.

We had something resembling the typical "January thaw" of the New England winter on the twenty-third. The air seemed to have a touch of springtime in it and there was open water about two miles to the south of us.

The next day we improved the time in overhauling the house that we had built out of boxes for the Eskimo, to make it more comfortable. Later on I was in the supply tent when I heard a confused noise in the galley. I waited a moment and then heard a tremendous racket of dishes rattling down and equipment being upset. I hurried out of the tent and into the galley. The canvas roof of the galley was on fire and parts of the rafters near the funnel. It was a pitch roof and around the funnel, where it passed through a hole in the roof, were a couple of tin collars and some asbestos. The cook had the stove pretty hot and as the canvas was dry and got overheated it had suddenly burst into flame. He was waving his arms around and trying to put the fire out with water and as he was very much in earnest about it he naturally did not always look to see where he was going and bumped violently into whatever happened to be in his way; hence the noise I had heard. A block of snow soon had the fire out.

McKinlay found a box of cocoa the same day and played a joke on us. When we were getting the emergency supplies overboard after the ship was struck I had given instructions that no tobacco should be saved, for I knew we could not afford to burden ourselves with a great supply of it on our sledge journeys later on and so we might as well get used to going without it as soon as possible. Some of the men happened to have some with them when they left the ship, however, and we smoked that while it lasted but it was already getting to be a scarce article. A good many odds and ends were continually turning up under the snow, however, and some of the men had an idea that if they looked for tobacco they might find some. So McKinlay set out to investigate.

In due time he returned, saying nothing but looking as if he knew something. We waited for him to hand over the tobacco or tell us where it was and at last we became so aroused that we made him guide us to the spot where he had been looking. He brought us to a place where a box was covered up in the snow, dug it up and handed it over, while we imagined the good smoke we were to have at last. It was a box of cocoa. McKinlay had the time of his life about it and we all laughed with him, though the joke was on us; I felt it incumbent on me, however, to show the joker that he couldn't trifle with our feelings with impunity, so I chased him laughing over the ice and scrubbed his face in a snowbank.

As a consolation prize I hunted through the supply tent for a little tobacco which I knew was there among the dunnage; I finally found it, divided it into small pieces and distributed it in that way to the whole party.

The chief engineer found some more treasure—two coffee percolators which were buried in the snow. When the cook tried to make coffee in them, however, he found that they wouldn't percolate.

Late in the day Chafe and Williams returned and reported no changes to mark in the trail, so far as they went.

CHAPTER XIV

THE SUN COMES BACK

January 25 was a day of rejoicing, because it marked the return of the sun, after seventy-one days. The sun was only rather indistinctly visible, half a disc above the ice, to the south, at noon, but from now on every day would be a little longer than the day before. It was the fourth time I had seen the sun come back in the Arctic and this time was the one which gave me the greatest satisfaction, because so much depended on our getting good daylight.

We celebrated by a little feast and some good singing in the evening. We had had a couple of cases of canned oysters on deck when the *Karluk* was struck and while I was waiting for the ship to go down on the eleventh I had found two tins of these oysters in the galley; the cook had brought them in to thaw them out. I threw the cases overboard on the ice where they broke and scattered tins of oysters around. We dug in the drifting snow and found this treasure trove and on this evening we had the oysters in soup and otherwise, and then had a "sing."

It was a fine clear night outside, with little or no wind, the land visible to the southwest and the temperature between thirty and forty below zero. Gathered around the big stove in the box-house we went through a varied and impromptu programme of song and recitation. Some one recited "Casey at the Bat," another "Lasca," while Munro gave us poems by Burns, of which he had a goodly store in his memory. With or without the accompaniment of instrumental music on a comb, we sang about every popular favorite, old and new: "Loch Lomond" and "The Banks of the Wabash," "The Heart Bowed Down" and "I Wonder Who's Kissing Her Now," "Sweet Afton" and "The Devil's Ball," "I Dreamt I Dwelt in Marble Halls" and "Maggie Murphy's Home," "Red Wing" (the favorite), "Aileen Alana" (another favorite), "Put on Your Old Gray Bonnet," "Alexander's Ragtime Band," "The Wearing of the Green," "Jingle Bells" (which might have been appropriate if we had used the dog harness which we had with bells on it and had ridden on the sledges instead of walking) and many another song, good, bad or indifferent. The Eskimo woman sang hymns and the little girl sang nursery songs, such as "Twinkle, Twinkle, Little Star," in which her mother joined.

It may be hard to believe but we were really enjoying ourselves these days. We were comfortable in our quarters, with plenty to eat and no lack of fuel. There was work to be done and all hands kept busily at it, with no time to mope or indulge in vain regrets; sleep came easily at the end of the day's occupations and though we did not have each man his private room and bath we had more soothing beds than I have slept on in some hotels.

Every day we progressed in our preparations to make the landward journey. On the twenty-sixth, for instance, in addition to the constant round of packing and repacking, weighing this and measuring that, we tested a couple of bell tents, which had been made on shipboard, to see if they were all right for use later on. Each had a pole going up through the middle; we found they were quite satisfactory and the men used them afterwards to live in on Wrangell Island.

On the twenty-seventh we got a view of the whole sun above the horizon and a good look at the land. In the half light of the previous days it had varied in size from time to time like a mirage and we could not tell whether it was Wrangell Island or not; now it seemed certain that it was not Wrangell so it must be Herald, according to the chart, a surmise which turned out to be correct.

"Herald Island,"—quoting again from the "Coast Pilot,"—"its highest point about 38 miles E. N. E. from Wrangell Island, was discovered

and landed upon by Capt. Kellett of H. M. S.
Herald, in 1849; it is about 4½ miles long N. W.
and S. E. and, being a solid mass of granite about
900 feet high, is almost inaccessible. Lieut.
Hooper, of the U. S. S. *Corwin,* also landed on it,
in 1881, and by barometer determined the height
of its highest peak, near the southeastern end, to
be 1200 feet."

Mr. Hadley and I got into an argument about
something—I never could recall just what it was—
and bet a good dinner on it, payable when we got
to Victoria. I remember that I lost the bet but
I still owe it, because when we finally reached Victoria many months later we had forgotten all about
it! Mr. Hadley was one of our most valuable
members because he could do so many things of
direct use to us in our emergency. He was the
oldest man of the party—fifty-seven—an English-
man by birth, who had left England when a lad and
been pretty much all over the world, in a variety
of occupations, which included a term of enlistment
in the United States navy.

I sent three men out on the twenty-eighth to see
how the trail made by the mate's and Mamen's parties was lasting; they returned late in the day and
reported an alteration and said that they had been
unable to pick up the trail again beyond the break.
So the next day I sent them out again, with Mr.

Hadley. They succeeded in picking up the trail and went as far as Mamen's first outward camp, about twelve miles from our main camp. I had told Mamen before he left that when it came near the time when I should be expecting him back I would build a big bonfire near Shipwreck Camp to guide him, one an hour before dark and another an hour after dark. We now carried out this programme, using altogether thirteen sacks of coal, a whaleboat and ten tins of gasoline. It gave out a big smoke. At night we opened a drum of alcohol and burned the canoe, besides three cases of gasoline.

January 30 was a beautiful day with little or no wind and a temperature not much below zero. Chafe, Williams and Maurer walked to Mamen's second camp and an hour and a half beyond it, returning about half past four to report that there were no alterations in the trail and that the going was good. They put up a flag at the point where they turned back. When the men went out on these short journeys over the ice they carried some supplies with them to cache along the trail for future use.

The next day Malloch, who was watchman, looked at the chronometer upside down so that the cook was late; he said that Malloch was his friend! I had intended to send Mr. Hadley and a party

away early to go to Mamen's third camp but he
did not get off until ten o'clock; with him were
Chafe, Williams, Maurer and Breddy. The party
returned about six and reported that they did not
reach the third camp but found good going and
believed the going good beyond; between Shipwreck Camp and Mamen's first camp the ice was
shifting a little. They said that they could see
our bonfire four miles away over the ice. I was
getting anxious about Mamen, for I had surely
looked to see him by the twenty-seventh.

After the Hadley party had left, the doctor and
Murray came to me and asked for supplies for
four men for fifty days, with a sledge, to go to the
land; they had been impatient to start for some
time. I told them that I should advise them to
wait with the rest of us and make the journey with
us when the conditions, which were improving all
the time as the light grew stronger, were right for
the final journey of the whole party. They did
not take kindly to my suggestion, however, but
felt that they would rather make the journey in
their own way, so I finally said that if they would
sign an agreement absolving me from all responsibility if they came to grief later on, I would give
them the supplies. They agreed to this. I told
them, furthermore, that if at any time they wanted
to come back to camp and rejoin the main party

they would be perfectly welcome to do so, and that if they required assistance later on I should be glad to do all in my power for them. Their party was to consist of four—the doctor, Murray, Beuchat and Sailor Morris. Morris went of his own accord, coming to me for permission to do so; I felt that he would be of use to them because he was a young man of twenty-six and handy, so I gave him the permission he desired. I offered the doctor's party their proportional share of the dogs, as soon as the dogs returned with Mamen, but they declined the offer, saying that they preferred to haul the sledge themselves.

The doctor's party began at once on the work of getting ready for their departure, assisted by McKinlay, who checked over their supplies with them. At the same time Chafe and Williams were getting ready to leave with a Peary sledge and four dogs to take supplies over Mamen's trail towards the land.

CHAPTER XV

February 3 dawned fine and clear. There were a few narrow leads of water near Shipwreck Camp; the ice was constantly cracking here and there around us as the wind veered and changed in velocity and as we were still drifting we heard many a crashing or grinding sound. Our own floe was intact, but wherever the ice opened beyond the edges of the floe the open water would make young ice again and this was not always heavy enough to withstand the constantly recurring pressure.

At half past eight Chafe and Williams left with a Peary sledge, four dogs and the following supplies, to leave at Mamen's fourth camp: eight tins of Hudson's Bay pemmican, one case of Underwood dog pemmican, two cases of biscuits, one case of coal oil, together with seventy days' food for themselves and the dogs, a camping outfit, empty pemmican tins and flags, to place on the ice rafters.

All day long we kept a lookout for Mamen and

124

his two Eskimo. About thirty yards away from the camp was a high rafter which we used as an observatory; every now and then while it was light, I was in the habit of going up there. Keruk, who was naturally anxious for the return of her husband, used to go up there, too, and as she had good eyesight I often asked her to go up and take a look.

Just before dark on the third—that is, about four o'clock—when we were most of us indoors, sewing or getting ready for dinner, Breddy came in and said that he believed Mamen was coming. We all rushed out. Keruk was up on the rafter but it was already too dark to see far. I could hear the dogs barking, however, and the voice of Kataktovick shouting to them. It was glorious. I ran down the trail and met the returning party coming along at a good pace. "Well done, Norway!" I shouted, shaking Mamen's hand and patting him on the back.

They came in to the camp, greeted with cheers, and we rushed them in and filled them up with hot coffee and biscuit. It was about dinner time and we put off dinner for about half an hour. The dogs, too, were hungry but I was ready for them with some pemmican and seal meat all cut up the day before and I fed them myself.

Nothing was said of their trip until after the

men had had their dinner; then Mamen related his experiences. They had made eleven marches going in, until they were stopped by open water three miles from land. He described the land which they saw and I made up my mind that it was not Wrangell Island but Herald Island, a conjecture which proved to be correct. They had had pretty good going, without the trouble with open leads and raftered ice which we had when we made our main journey later on.

They had reached the edge of the open water January 31 without untoward incident, though one of their dogs had run away and King had frozen his heel. Mamen and the Eskimo had stayed with the shore party a day and had left on February 1 for their return to Shipwreck Camp. The mate, he said, had decided to land as soon as the lead closed up; this worried me a good deal because the mate and his party were not familiar with travel over the young ice and, besides that, Herald Island is no place for a party to land upon, for it is inaccessible, owing to its precipitous sides, and, according to American government reports, has no driftwood on its shores. In fact it has practically no shore to speak of, excepting one short stretch; it is simply a rocky islet. Up to the time when Mamen left there was no chance to land on the island and Mamen hardly thought that the mate's party would be able to land there. I hoped that they would keep on to Wrangell Island and carry out their instructions.

Mamen's journey back to camp was much faster than the shoreward journey, because they had more light and could sleep in the igloos they had built going in. The last day back they had made a wonderful march, leaving their igloo at the earliest twilight and coming all day; they had not even stopped to eat since they had broken camp. They had relieved each other at driving the dogs.

As soon as they got their clothing well dried out, I decided to send Mamen and the Eskimo back to the island to locate the mate's party. At the same time they could move supplies along the trail, for now that the road was made, the going would be easier.

The evening of the fourth Murray came to me and said that the doctor's party planned to leave the next day. The fifth opened clear and calm and the doctor, Murray, Beuchat and Morris got away about nine o'clock, hauling their sledge-load of supplies along the trail.

Later on Chafe and Williams got in. They had landed their supplies safely at the fourth camp and set to work at once, drying out their clothing and, with the help of all the rest of us, preparing for the next shoreward trip. On the way back to the camp they had passed the doctor and his companions, all in good spirits and looking forward to any but the unhappy fate that was to overtake them.

Before the doctor's party left they handed me the following letter:

CANADIAN ARCTIC EXPEDITION,
Sunday, Feb. 1st, 1914.

Captain Robert Bartlett,

SIR: We, the undersigned, in consideration of the present critical situation, desire to make an attempt to reach the land. We ask you to assist us by issuing to us from the general stores all necessary sledging and camping provisions and equipment for the proposed journey as per separate requisition already handed to you. On the understanding that you do so and continue as heretofore to supply us with our proportional share of provisions while we remain in camp, and in the event of our finding it necessary to return to the camp, we declare that we undertake the journey on our own initiative and absolve you from any responsibility whatever in the matter.

A. FORBES MACKAY   H. BEUCHAT
JAMES MURRAY   S. S. MORRIS

Their supplies consisted of the following: one Nome sledge, one Burberry tent, 96 pounds of Underwood pemmican, 112 pounds of Hudson's Bay pemmican, 138 pounds of biscuit, four tins of Horlick's malted milk, 30 pounds of sugar, four boxes of tabloid tea, 16 tins of cocoa, 52 cakes of

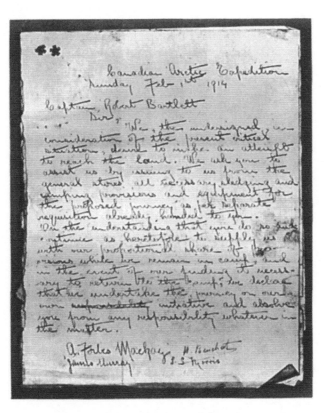

LETTER FROM THE DOCTOR'S PARTY TO
CAPTAIN BARTLETT

chocolate, six gallons of coal oil, one quart of alcohol, one Primus stove and outfit, four mugs, four spoons, one spade, one ice axe, one hatchet, one Mannlicher rifle and 100 rounds of ammunition, 20 yards of rope, one dozen candles, one package of matches, five pounds of butter, one tent floor and a tracing of Wrangell Island from the chart. These supplies were sufficient for fifty days.

The cook was up at four on the morning of the seventh and we breakfasted at half past five. At 6:15 Chafe and Williams left for the fifth camp with a sledge-load of supplies, consisting of 96 pounds of Underwood pemmican, 80 pounds of Hudson's Bay pemmican, one case of oil, seven days' food for themselves and their dogs and a camping outfit. At seven Mamen and the two Eskimo got away, with three sledges and seventeen dogs. Their sledges were loaded with four cases of Underwood man pemmican, three cases of dog pemmican, each case containing forty-eight pounds, three cases of oil, ten cases of biscuit and 256 pounds of Hudson's Bay pemmican; they were to pick up supplies enough at the fourth camp to give them 1800 pounds' weight for their three sledges. They were then to go on and look for the mate's party and leave one sledge and the supplies as far in as they could along the trail, bringing back the other two sledges light.

Mamen could report on the condition of the trail and keep it open and at the same time carry out the essential part of my plan of getting the supplies well along towards the land in advance of the main party. If he should fail to find the mate's party, the assumption was that they had gone on to Wrangell Island.

At 2 P. M. Mamen came back to the camp; with him was Williams. When some distance along the way Mamen had dislocated his knee-cap, which had already been dislocated when he was ski-jumping in Norway. He had been going on, however, in spite of his accident, when he met Chafe and Williams returning. Williams had fallen through the young ice about four miles out and they had decided to return so that he could get his clothing dried out, when they met Mamen. The latter had told Chafe of his accident and it was decided that he and Williams should come back to camp while Chafe took over the command of Mamen's party and went on towards the island.

I was busy about the camp when I heard them coming. I knew that something must be wrong and went out to meet them. Mamen was riding on the sledge and Williams was running to keep warm, for the temperature was about thirty-five degrees below zero and he had got pretty wet in getting out of the water. I rushed them into the box-house where Williams had some hot tea and changed his clothes. Then I sent him, with the chief engineer, to overtake Chafe and continue on the shoreward journey.

Williamson, the second engineer, worked over Mamen's knee, massaged it and finally got the knee-cap back into place. It was hard work because it kept slipping out of the socket and had to be bandaged with surgeon's plaster to keep it in place. In fact it was not until the tenth that Mamen got so that he could hobble around and the dislocation was very painful.

Sunday, the eighth, I took stock of our pemmican and found that we had 4,932 pounds left in camp; we had used up and sledged along the trail some 5,000 pounds. We ate no pemmican in camp, and fed the dogs mostly on seal meat excepting when on the march. Most of the dogs were now out and we had in camp only those which were crippled or otherwise incapacitated.

Shortly after noon on the ninth Mr. Munro and Williams came in. They had been held up by open water between the second and third camps and had been unable to overtake Chafe and the Eskimo. The next day they had started on the march again, only to be held up again by open water; late in the afternoon, however, the ice had closed up so that they could go on to the fifth camp.

Here they could not find a heavy enough floe to
build a cache on so they had returned and put off
the load at the fourth camp, which was on a large
heavy floe, an ideal place for a cache.

Munro left camp again early on the morning of
the eleventh, with Malloch, four dogs, seven cases
of pemmican, a camping outfit and food for seven
days. They were to go beyond the fifth camp and
leave the pemmican at the best place they could
find. The temperature was 38 degrees below zero,
the weather fine and clear.

The next day, however, was dull and cloudy,
with a fresh northeast wind and a falling barometer. It looked as if our fine weather would soon
be over and I feared that the different parties out
on the trail would be storm-bound. Towards
night the wind came on strong east, and continued
so through the following day; I was sorry to
see this for we should be set towards the west if it
continued. The next day, however, was a beautiful day; the air was clear and frosty, with little or
no wind. The land was distinctly visible and I
thought I could see Wrangell Island to the southwest. It was St. Valentine's Day and Bob, the
cook, sent two of the men valentines of soup adver-
tisements.

About noon the chief engineer and Malloch came
in. They were in a sorry condition. They had

spent a most uncomfortable night walking about on the ice to keep warm, for late in the afternoon while trying to make quick time they got on to some thin ice and Munro broke through. The sledge began to sink but fortunately Munro got out all right and they held the sledge up long enough to cut the pemmican away. The pemmican was, of course, all lost and their clothes and camping outfit were saturated. The stove was damaged in the accident and they had nothing to warm themselves with. We got them fixed up at once and then cleaned off the sledge and loaded it again, for Breddy and Maurer were to go to the fourth camp the next day.

It was my turn to be watchman that night and I spent a good part of the time studying the chart. From our present position Herald Island seemed to be about sixty miles away.

Breddy and Maurer left on the fifteenth with seven cases of pemmican to go over the trail to the fourth camp.

The next afternoon at four o'clock Chafe and the Eskimo came in. They were heartily welcomed. Chafe reported that he got to a point within three miles of Herald Island when he was held up by open water. In fact for two days he and his party were adrift on a small sheet of ice in a three-mile lead. They were close enough to the island to see the land clearly and in detail but though he looked constantly with binoculars he could see no one on the island nor any tent or other indication that men were there, so he concluded that the mate and his party had carried out their orders and gone on to Wrangell Island. This seemed likely to me and I hoped that it was so. The Eskimo had improved the time in shooting and succeeded in getting four seal.

On the way back the trail was faulted in places and the party had difficulty in finding it. When about twenty miles from Herald Island on their return trip they had come upon the Mackay party, struggling towards the land. Mackay, Murray and Morris were drawing the sledge; Beuchat was a mile and a half behind, with hands and feet frozen and partly delirious from suffering. Morris had cut his left hand with a knife and blood-poisoning had already set in. Chafe's opinion was that Beuchat would die that night. He said that Beuchat expressed his sorrow that he had left the main party. The Mackay party had taken their pemmican out of the tins before they left Shipwreck Camp and put it all in a bag; in going over some young ice their sledge had got into the water and the bag of pemmican had got wet. Altogether they were in bad shape. Chafe offered them

assistance. They declined it and said they were
bound for Wrangell Island. They did accept some
seal meat which Chafe had. Munro and Malloch
had spoken the Mackay party earlier on their
march and so had Chafe himself, when he had first
started out, but their condition had then been good,
though they had been making slow progress, and
each party had tried to persuade them to return
to Shipwreck Camp.

Chafe reported that he had left all his supplies
at the sixth camp, excepting just enough to take
him back to Shipwreck Camp. He had lost one
dog and had had to leave a broken sledge along
the way.

Maurer and Breddy came in soon after Chafe
arrived; they reported that they had left their load
safely at the fourth camp. All hands, except the
four men of the mate's party and the four of the
doctor's, were now assembled once more at Shipwreck Camp.

It was a severe disappointment to me not to have
word of the safety of the mate and his party. I
had thought that they might possibly return with
Chafe and be with us on our final march to the
island which I was now planning to get under way
at once.

We had a northeast gale on the seventeenth

CHAPTER XVI

On the morning of February 19, I called the cook at four o'clock, so that we had an early breakfast for the start of the advance guard.

There were two parties, each with a sledge and four dogs. In the first party were Malloch, Hadley, Williamson and Breddy; in the second Munro, Maurer, Williams and Chafe. Each party would have man-harness to help out the dogs when necessary.

On the first party's sledge were six cases of man pemmican, two cases of biscuit, two gallons of oil, 84 tins of milk, 2,400 tea tablets in tins hermetically sealed, one Mannlicher rifle, 250 rounds of ammunition, one Ross revolver (Malloch's own), 400 rounds of ammunition, one Primus stove, one gallon of alcohol, 500 22-calibre cartridges, one 401 Winchester, 100 rounds of ammunition, one pair of ski, matches, a pickaxe, hatchets, sleeping-robes and a tent. On the other sledge were five cases of man pemmican, two cases of biscuit, 84 tins of milk, two gallons of oil, one gallon of alcohol, 2,400 tea tablets, one Primus stove, one Mannlicher rifle,

250 rounds of ammunition, matches, pick-axe, hatchets, a tent, snow-shoes and a tracing of the map of Wrangell Island. Every man had a new suit of Jaeger underwear given him. The parties were to pick up supplies along the trail so that they would thus be replacing supplies used on the march, and take full loads with them in to the land. For this march was to take these eight men clear through to Wrangell Island and they were saying good-by to Shipwreck Camp for good. The men shook hands all around and got away about eight o'clock in the morning.

On one of the sledges they had a passenger. While we were fitting out the ship at the navy yard at Esquimault, some one presented us with a cat, as black as the ace of spades. She was kept in the forecastle at first; after a while she got aft and Mr. Hadley became greatly interested in her, training her to do tricks. When the ship was crushed and we were working to get things out of her before she sank I told the men to be sure not to forget the cat, but to put her in a basket and place her in the box-house. There she became very much at home. Early in her residence she got into difficulties with a dog, that had wandered through the entrance, by landing suddenly like an animated bunch of porcupine quills on the dog's nose. The dog shook her off and tried to take his revenge. We saved the cat just in time. After that she never bothered the dogs again. When the advance party now started for the land Hadley and Maurer made a deer-skin bag to carry the cat and she rode on a sledge in state. Her food consisted chiefly of pemmican scraps.

With the rest of the party and all the supplies we could carry, I had intended to start the day after the earlier party. Kerdrillo, however, was in no condition to travel. He had hurt his back going in to Herald Island and it gave him a good deal of pain, so it seemed wise to wait until he was better. We had two lame dogs and the delay on account of Kerdrillo would give them, too, a chance to recuperate. Ice travel is as hard on dogs as on men and, besides that, the dogs were always fighting among themselves, if they were not sharply watched, and one of them had so bad a tear in his leg that Mamen had to take nine stitches in it, using the regulation surgical needle and silk thread. We had twelve dogs left besides Nellie, one of the dogs that had had pups. We had built a snow-house for her and her pups, but as it was clear that the pups would not be of service to us now, we had to have them killed to save Nellie's strength. She improved enough to be of value later on.

For several days while we waited we had a high

easterly gale and snowdrift. I wondered how the eight men of the advance guard were getting along and what they thought had become of the rest of us. Daily I had to rub poor Kerdrillo's back and put plasters on it. His improvement was slow but fortunately his condition was not the only bar to our immediate departure, for the weather was too bad for efficient travel and it was far better for us to be eating supplies in camp where we had plenty than to be consuming them detained by the storm in some igloo along the trail. We fed the dogs seal meat, for we had several seal left, and also pemmican, for we still had plenty of that, and I was feeding the dogs all they would eat, to get them in as good condition as possible for the final march. This would be continuous travel with little sleep and now, on account of the storm, hard going and extra work in locating the trail.

The Eskimo occupied some of their time in camp fitting up harpoons and spears to save ammunition. They also put our snowshoes in good condition and spliced hatchet-handles on to the handles of the snow-knives so that they could wield them better in cutting out snow-blocks for igloos.

The supply-tent was all snowed under, but by digging around I succeeded in getting out a few things that I wanted. We all had a shave and a bath and changed our underclothing. I used a fork to comb my hair for I had given my comb to Keruk; it is surprising what an excellent comb a fork makes,—I recommend it for Arctic use.

There was just a little tobacco left. Mamen found a small piece of chewing-tobacco under the boards. Keruk, whom we all called "Auntie," had a little and when I wanted tobacco I would ask Auntie for a pipeful.

On the twenty-third the storm was breaking at last. Huge banks of snow were piled high around the camp; we were all snowed in. The two crippled dogs were in the box-house with us; the other dogs were in the snow-igloo, which had been occupied by the men who had now gone to the land. It took us nearly all day on the twenty-third to dig our way through the snow from the box-house to the igloo in order to feed the dogs. We dug the supply tent out and busied ourselves getting ready for our departure. In fact we stayed up all night, giving the final touches to our clothing.

At 4 A. M. on February twenty-fourth we had coffee and began loading our sledges. As soon as Kerdrillo's sledge, a remodeled Nome sledge, was loaded I started him off. With him went his wife and their two children, and Templeman, the cook. Keruk carried her baby, Mugpi, on her back all the way to Wrangell Island; the older girl covered the entire distance on foot, sometimes even helping her father with the sledge. Kerdrillo had five dogs. His sledge was loaded with four cases of man pemmican, forty-eight tins of milk, two tins of biscuit, one case of oil, 2,400 tea tablets, in hermetically sealed tins, one 30.30 Winchester rifle, 200 rounds of ammunition, one tent, one Primus stove, one axe, two pickaxes, candles, a gallon of alcohol, matches, snow-knives and sleeping robes.

The rest of us had two sledges, one with three dogs, driven by Kataktovick, the other with four dogs, driven by myself. On Kataktovick's sledge were three cases of man pemmican, thirty-six cases of milk, two cases of biscuit, ten gallons of oil and 2,400 tea tablets. My own sledge carried four cases of man pemmican, two cases of biscuit, thirty-six cases of milk, twelve tins of coal oil, 2,400 tea tablets, one tent, matches, one Primus stove, one axe, two pickaxes, candles, snow-knives, one gallon of alcohol, one pair of snowshoes, one pair of ski, one Mannlicher rifle, 250 rounds of ammunition, one Colt revolver, 100 rounds of ammunition, sleeping-robes, rope and spare harness. We had to leave a Peary sledge in camp because there were not dogs enough to make a team to haul it. As it was, our three sledges, with their four-hundred-pound loads, were heavily burdened for the dogs we had, with some of them in a half-crippled condition.

MUGPI

"Keruk carried her baby, Mugpi, on her back all the way
to Wrangell Island. *See page 141*

At about noon we finally got away—Katakto-vick, McKinlay, Mamen and I. McKinlay, wearing man-harness, helped pull my sledge, while I guided and drove the dogs. On account of his dislocated knee-cap which bothered him constantly and once on the march got out of place and had to be put back, with strenuous efforts on my part and much silent suffering on his, Mamen could not help pull Kataktovick's sledge but had to limp alongside and make his way as best he could. He chafed very much over his temporary uselessness and I had to cheer him up as well as I could by telling him constantly what wonderful work he had already accomplished.

We placed a record in a copper tank on the ice, telling where the ship was lost and when we left camp, with the names of the members of the various parties as they had left. In camp and on the ice we left behind us two transits, about 3,000 pounds of pemmican, 80 cases of biscuit, 200 sacks of coal, ten cases of gasoline, two drums of coal oil, with various odds and ends; over the camp we left the British ensign flying. I had my charts with me. On the day we left, on account of a sudden clearing up of the atmosphere and a temporary cessation of the almost continuous whirling snowdrift, I had a good view of Wrangell Island, the first sure view I had had of it.

We had reached a point beyond the second camp by nightfall. Here we stopped. We had intended to make the third camp, but it was getting very dark, we had been up all the previous night, had worked hard all day and were very tired, so we were forced to pitch our tents and had to spend a miserable night under canvas. The tent was not large enough for us, yet all four of us occupied it and our breathing filled it with condensation. Our dogs, too, were rather sluggish the first day out, for they had been well stuffed with food during the time of our enforced delay in camp.

We welcomed daylight the next morning and turned out at four o'clock, and after our standard ration of tea, biscuit and pemmican, were soon on the march. All hands were glad to be off and the dogs, too, worked better than on the first day, so we made good progress. In most places the road had been destroyed by the storm of the past few days, so the work of the preliminary sledging parties was of little use to us, though sometimes we could make out where the trail led; chiefly, however, we had to make our own way, guided by the empty pemmican tins and flags, where these still stayed up, and by the sight of Wrangell Island to the southwest. We managed to keep the general direction of the travelled road from camp to camp,

SHIPWRECK CAMP

" We placed a record in a copper tank on the ice, telling where the ship was lost and when we left camp, with the names of the members of the various parties as they had left. . . Over the camp we left the British ensign flying." *See page 143*

though it often took time and care to study out the
way to go.

At the fourth camp I found a note from Munro
saying that they had been held up there by open
water and a heavy gale, the same, evidently, which
had detained us at Shipwreck Camp, and that they
had shot a polar bear near by. This I knew even
before I read the note for I found a big piece of
bear-meat that they had left in the igloo for us.
They had been unable to take all the pemmican
at the cache here along with them; we picked up
a few tins of it but could not take any more, for
we were already overburdened.

Munro's note further said that the trail beyond
was badly smashed but we went on as fast as we
could, for we wanted to catch up with Kerdrillo and
I was anxious to know that the advance party was
continuing to get along well. At quarter past
four we reached the sixth igloo. These camps were
from four to ten miles apart. We found at this
camp five gallons of oil, which the advance party
left, three cases of pemmican, four cases of biscuit and some alcohol. There should have been
another cache near by but the ice had raftered
under pressure of the recent storm and destroyed
it, thereby losing us a lot of biscuit and pemmican,
and, what was just then even more valuable, perhaps, twelve gallons of oil.

At half past four we finally came up with Kerd-rillo and his party. We had made the thirty miles from Shipwreck Camp to the sixth camp in two days, going twelve the first day and eighteen the second. Kerdrillo and his family were already occupying the igloo at this camp so we built another for ourselves.

In building a snow-igloo the first thing to do is to find a level place where the ice is heavy and will not crack; it is of course not always possible to find the ideal spot and you have to be content with the heaviest ice you can find and take your chances. The snow should be hard and firmly packed. You start in cutting blocks of snow with a snow-knife, an implement which has a steel blade about a foot and a half long, two inches wide and a sixteenth of an inch thick, with a wooden handle about six inches long, an inch and a half wide and a quarter of an inch thick; we had lengthened the handles of our snow-knives by lashing hatchet-handles to them, as I have already mentioned, so that we could use both hands in wielding them. Sometimes instead of a snow-knife we would use an ordinary hand-saw in cutting the blocks out; we could often do more work with this than with a snow-knife. The Eskimo in the distant past used to use a knife made of stone or bone.

The size of the snow-blocks varied. For the

lower tiers of the walls of the igloo we used blocks as large as could be cut without breaking; for the upper tiers the size was somewhat smaller, tapering off to the roof. The blocks varied in thickness from a foot and a half to two feet, according to the condition of the snow. A properly completed igloo is round, with a conical roof which requires considerable skill and practice to make. It took our Eskimo a long time, however, to cover in the roof, so we used to use the tent we had with us for the roof, with our snowshoes and ski for a tent-pole. Our igloos were square instead of round. Inside we would build a bed-platform of snow, large enough for us all to sleep on; we would place our fur sleeping-robes on this platform and lie down to sleep. We slept in our clothes, with no covering over us; it is not safe to use sleeping-bags on the sea-ice for when the ice cracks underneath you, the sleeping-bags hobble your arms and legs and you drown. We never caught cold; in fact "colds" and pneumonia do not exist in the Arctic beyond the limit of habitation of civilized man.

When we got our igloo built we would make a half-circular opening in one of the sides and crawl in; then we would fill up this opening with a snow-block, cut down to fit it tightly enough to make it air-proof. For ventilation we had small holes punched in the walls. Once inside we would light our Primus stove and make our tea, eat our biscuit and pemmican by candlelight, lie down and go to sleep.

We were not ordinarily troubled with insomnia, but sometimes, like a peaceful community the night before the Fourth, we were kept awake in spite of ourselves. Between ten and eleven on the night of the twenty-fifth, for instance, the ice began to crack in the vicinity of our camp and from time to time we in our igloo would feel severe shocks, as of an earthquake. Through the snow walls I could hear the Eskimo out on the ice. Kataktovick went out to see what was up and came back at once to tell me that a crack two or three feet wide had opened through the middle of Kerdrillo's igloo, which was about five yards away from ours, and that they had nearly lost their little baby but fortunately had got out before anything happened to them.

The ice continued to crack about us all through the night. There was no crack in our igloo so I gave it to Keruk and her children for the rest of the night and we walked back and forth, waiting for daylight. It was not very dark for the stars were shining brilliantly. The temperature was about forty below zero. All around us the ice was breaking and at times we were on a floating island.

As soon as daylight came I sent McKinlay and

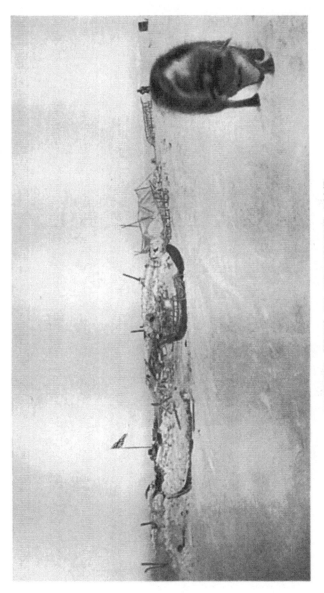

ANOTHER VIEW OF SHIPWRECK CAMP

Kataktovick, with all the dogs and an empty sledge, back to Shipwreck Camp for about thirty gallons of the oil that we had left there. They had all the dogs from the three sledges and could make good progress.

While McKinlay and Kataktovick were gone Kerdrillo and I went on a scouting tour ahead for a way to see how the road looked. We found that the storm had destroyed the old trail and that the trail newly made by the Munro-Hadley party was already changed somewhat, though as yet not very much. While we were on this scout Kerdrillo caught a glimpse, through our binoculars, of two men of the advance party, just visible against the sky-line on a high rafter eight or ten miles away. When we came back to camp, I had Kerdrillo build another igloo for his party. During the day the ice had all closed up again.

About half past three the next afternoon McKinlay and Kataktovick returned from Shipwreck Camp, with thirty gallons of oil, two tins of alcohol, twelve sealskins, a few fawnskins and 6,000 tea tablets. They said that both ways they had found our trail unaltered; apparently the only movement of the ice had been at the sixth camp, where we were.

CHAPTER XVII

At dawn the next morning, February 28, leaving at this sixth camp some cases of biscuits, with alcohol and coal oil, we started again landward, going over the trail made by the advance party. At one P. M. we came up with them. They were halted by a huge conglomeration of raftered ice tossed up by the storm which had delayed us at Shipwreck Camp. The rafters were from twenty-five to a hundred feet high and ran directly across our path, parallel to the land, and extending in either direction as far as the eye could reach. Viewed from an ice pinnacle high enough to give a clear sight across in the direction of the land the mass of broken ice looked to be at least three miles wide. To get around it was clearly out of the question; an attempt to do so might lead us no one knew whither. Clearly it was a case for hard labor, to build a road across it practicable for sledging; I had seen similar apparently impassible ice on our polar trips but never anything worse. At three o'clock, therefore, I told all hands to set to work building igloos and said that to-morrow we would

begin with pickaxes to make a road across the
rafters. While they were building the igloos I
made a reconnaissance ahead for some distance, returning about dark. We had no thermometer, so
that we could not tell the exact temperature, but
from the condition of the coal oil, which was very
thick and viscid, it must have been between forty-
five and fifty-five below zero. It was excellent
weather for sledging, fine, clear and calm, if the
going had only been good.

March 1, at daylight, I sent back Chafe and
Mamen, with an empty sledge and ten dogs, to
bring up all the oil, biscuit and alcohol that remained at the sixth camp. They returned with a
well-laden sledge, late in the afternoon. I discovered during the day that Malloch and Maurer
had frozen their feet, a thing which caused them a
good deal of suffering and me a good deal of
anxiety. Men with frozen feet are seriously handicapped and make the progress of all difficult until
they recover. Fortunately in the present instance
the men made known their predicament soon
enough to be relieved before dangerously frost-
bitten.

At daylight the next morning I sent McKinlay,
Hadley and Chafe back over the trail again, to go
clear through to Shipwreck Camp with an empty
sledge and fourteen dogs. They were to bring

back the Peary sledge that we had left there and full loads of pemmican, biscuit and tea.

Our work at road-making which we had begun the day before, was progressing steadily. It was cold, seemingly endless labor, for almost every foot of the trail had to be hewn out of the ice to make a path three or four feet wide, smoothed off enough to permit our sledges to be drawn over it without being smashed. By three o'clock in the afternoon we had got over the first big chain of ridges and on to a small level floe. We were still far from the other side of the great rafters but by working diligently could feel that we had accomplished something at last. We worked on a little too long before starting back to camp and darkness was almost upon us. So I asked the cook to go back to camp while the rest of us were finishing our day's work and tell Keruk and Malloch and Maurer that we were coming and wanted to have hot tea ready for us as soon as we got back. Malloch and Maurer had been compelled by their frozen feet to rest for the time being, though they insisted that they be allowed to do their share of the work and I almost had to use force to keep them quiet.

The rest of us finally knocked off work and made our way back over the rather tortuous road but when we reached camp no preparations had been made to give us our much-needed tea and on inquiry I found that Templeman had not turned up. It was now almost dark and I was a good deal concerned about his absence, for though a splendid cook and as willing a worker as a man could be, he was not strong enough to withstand for very long the hardships that would surround him if he were lost on the ice. I set out to look for him and we fired off guns and shouted and altogether made all the noise we could to attract his attention. Finally to my great relief I saw him floundering through the snow on a big floe about a quarter of a mile from the camp. My revulsion of feeling was like that of an anxious parent who thinks his youngster has gone off and got lost and then discovers him making his way homeward. In the parable the prodigal son receives the fatted calf; in practice I fear that most errant youngsters receive a sound spanking and perhaps do not suspect until years later that this disguises a tremendous feeling of joy, which expresses itself perversely in punishment for recklessness and warnings "never to do it again." So when I espied poor Templeman my first impulse was to berate him soundly for wandering from the narrow, though none too straight, path back to camp but when I got near enough to see that he was wading through snow, into which he sank to the waist at every step, and had had the good sense to keep his pickaxe with him, though he

graphs here but somehow when the light was good enough and I had the time, my camera would be back in camp and when I had my camera with me we would be on the march and I had no time to play photographer. Taking pictures was no sinecure on this trip, anyway, because the cold seemed to affect the shutter and the unrolling of the films. If George Borup had been with us as he was with Peary on our North Pole trip, what a great collection of photographs he could have taken!

March 4, at about four P. M., we finished working through the rafter and came out on the smoother ice on its landward side. Mamen, Kataktovick and I spent the day sledging supplies across from the camp on the farther side and when the road was finished we all went back for the last load. It was not until eight P. M. that we had all our supplies at the new camp and we had to do the last of the work in the dark; the Eskimo had built three igloos while we were sledging. It had taken us four days to get across a distance of three miles. From the shore side it was easy to see the basis of the formation of such rafters. A storm causes the moving ice to smash against and slide over the still ice and the pressure of the "irresistible force meeting the immovable body" throws the ice into fantastic, mountainous formations that are as weird as that astounding picture of Chaos before the Creation that used to ornament the first volume of Ridpath's "History of the World."

At daylight on March 5 I sent Munro and a party back across the three miles of raftered ice to meet the McKinlay party who were about due back from Shipwreck Camp. Munro and the others could guide and help them across the difficult road we had made. While they were gone I took Kataktovick and laid out a trail towards the land for the next day's march. Now for the first time since we left Shipwreck Camp, we got a view of Wrangell Island; it was high and we seemed almost under it. The air was exceptionally clear and the land looked close to us.

Munro and his party did not get back until long after dark. They had reached our last camp across the raftered ice and not finding McKinlay and the others there had continued on the back trail, hoping to meet them. They went on as far as they could go without being compelled to stay out all night, and then came back, because they had no sleeping-robes and would have had a poor night of it, besides being obliged to build an igloo. They were wise in knowing when they had gone far enough; Munro showed his usual good judgment.

Our progress in to the island was retarded by the necessity of keeping along with us as large a quantity of supplies as possible. This meant relaying supplies, because the going was bad and made sledging difficult, with the small number of dogs we had. On the sixth, as soon as the first streak of light appeared, I sent Munro and his party back again to meet the McKinlay party, while I took Kataktovick and Kerdrillo and went ahead towards the island, road-making with our pickaxes. Munro had told me that when he first saw the three-mile belt of raftered ice, he never thought for a moment that we should ever get through it. Any novice certainly had a right to feel discouraged; it was as tough a job as I ever tackled. We now picked our way—I might almost say pick-axed our way—across the ice from our last camp for a distance of seven miles until we came to a large, heavy floe, which would make a good place for a new camp; here we threw off the light loads which we had brought on two of the Peary sledges and returned to camp. At half past four the McKinlay party came in, convoyed by Munro and his party. McKinlay and his companions had gone clear back to Shipwreck Camp and brought in six cases of dog pemmican, sixteen cases of Hudson's Bay pemmican, thirty gallons of gasoline, and some hatchets and snow-knives. They had left at the first camp from Shipwreck Camp four cases of Underwood dog pemmican and ten tins of Hudson's Bay pem-

plies ten miles nearer the land, returning to the igloos on the big floe for the night. We found that at one of the temporary caches along the way two bears had destroyed a case of coal oil and scattered two tins of biscuit over the ice.

It was hard luck, after getting the oil so near the island, to have bears to contend with in addition to the elements, especially as our dogs were not trained to follow a bear, so that there was no use trying to go after them. A polar bear has a very acute sense of smell and can scent a human being in plenty of time to get away from him, and as a bear can go faster than a man it can escape easily, unless the hunter has dogs trained from puppyhood to follow a bear and round him up, the way the dogs of Greenland can do. Of the bears that the McKinlay party shot the meat was simply cut off the bones, to have no useless weight to carry and some of it was cached on the ice, with the skins, and the rest brought with us. We expected to be able to get it later on but never did because we did not go back over the trail again, and we expected to get more bears on our way to the island.

On the tenth we kept up the task of sledging the supplies forward. We worked from daylight to dark, some with pickaxes, others with sledges with light loads, for the going was rough. The Eskimo built the igloos and by night we had all our supplies up, Munro, Mamen and myself getting in with the last load just at dark.

The going was bad nearly all the way along here. Kataktovick and I were off at the first crack of dawn picking the trail for the others to follow with their pickaxes and their lightly loaded sledges. It was necessary for us to make fairly good loads, for a white man can not handle a sledge as deftly as an Eskimo can and we had not enough Eskimo to drive all the sledges even if they had been free from the work of trail-making and building igloos.

We made about seven miles during the day. Sometimes we had to get the sledges up on a ridge fifty feet high with an almost sheer drop on the other side. When we came to such rough paces we would harness all the dogs to a sledge and all of us who could get a hand on it would help push the sledge. When we got the sledge up to the top we would run a rope from it to another sledge down below and as the first sledge went down the other side it would pull the second sledge up.

CHAPTER XVIII

March 12 we got away again at dawn. Mc-Kinlay, Mamen, Kataktovick, Kerdrillo and his family and I went ahead of the others, with lightly loaded sledges, and, on account of improved ice conditions, made such good progress that at one P. M. we landed on Icy Spit, on the northeast side of Wrangell Island. It is perhaps easier to imagine than to describe our feelings of relief at being once again on *terra firma,* after two months of drifting and travelling on the ice. We had had a hard road to travel much of the way from Ship-wreck Camp, but fortunately, since the big storm in the days following the departure of the advance party, we had had continuously fine weather, with good daylight and exhilarating temperatures in the minus forties and fifties.

As soon as we landed we began building an igloo. There was plenty of driftwood scattered all about and Keruk gathered up a lot of it and built a fire, so that by the time the first of our three igloos was built she had some tea for us and the rest of the party who, coming along easily with light loads

161

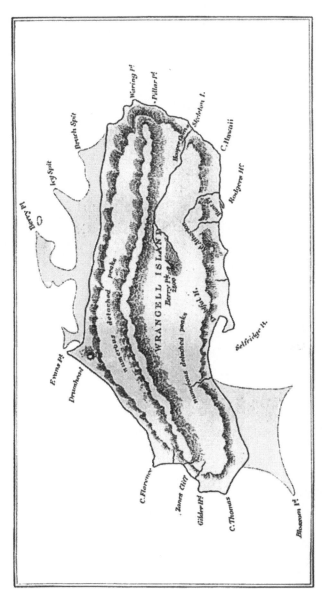

MAP OF WRANGELL ISLAND

"March 12 we got away again at dawn . . . and made such good progress that at one p. m. we landed on Icy Spit, on the northeast side of Wrangell Island. It is perhaps easier to imagine than to describe our feelings of relief at being once again on *terra firma*, after two months of drifting and travelling on the ice."

See page 161

over our trail, arrived an hour and a half after we did. We were overjoyed to find the driftwood for, although we were pretty sure of finding it, yet we were a little dubious and it was a great relief to my mind to know that fuel was assured.

We could see a good deal of the island from the spit, which made out from land some distance into the ocean. Waring Point lay far to the east of us and Evans Point to the west. The geographical names on Wrangell Island are derived from the names of the officers of the U. S. S. *Rodgers* who explored the island in 1881. On a clear day like this it was not unusual to be able to see for seventy miles. The northeast side of the island, on which we now were, sent several low sandy spits out from the land, thus forming lagoons which of course were covered with ice. Near the coast were low mountains and valleys, with higher peaks in the interior beyond. Here and there on the beach were dead trees that had drifted ashore, with the roots sticking up into the air; we also found planks and other lumber. Everything was snowclad and white, only a degree less cheerless than the frozen ocean itself.

The next day Munro, Chafe, Breddy and Williams went back with all the dogs and sledges to the last camp on the ice, fifteen miles from our landing-place, and brought in all the supplies we

had left there. While they were gone I sent Kerdrillo nine miles across the lagoon to Berry Spit,
to see if he could find any traces of the mate's party
or the Mackay party. He took his rifle with him to
look for game. When he came back at nightfall,
he reported that he had seen no traces of either
party and only one bear track and one fox track.
This was an indication that there was small chance
of getting a bear on or near the island, because
there were no seal holes within twenty-five miles
from land; we had seen some near the big rafter,
about forty miles out. Later in the season, as the
ice broke up nearer the land, the seal would work
in shore and of course the bears would follow. I
asked Kerdrillo what he thought the chances were
of there being any caribou or reindeer on the island.
It is not an uncommon thing to find caribou on
islands in Hudson Strait, which have drifted on
the ice from the mainland, and there were, I knew,
both these animals in plenty on the Siberian coast.
I wondered, too, whether there might not be Arctic
hare on the island. Kerdrillo said he thought there
was so much snow that caribou and reindeer would
be unlikely to stay where it would be so difficult
for them to get food and he did not believe any
were to be found.

The next day, to verify his opinion, I sent him
out again, giving him tea and pemmican, so that he

could have a full day's march and make a reconnaissance into the interior. About dark he returned
and reported that he had seen no traces of caribou,
reindeer or hare and very few signs of foxes.
Later on, however, he thought ptarmigan would
visit the island. He had seen one bear track,
which he thought was about three days old, probably of the bear whose tracks he had seen on the
previous day.

The story is told of a student who, when asked
to name five Arctic animals, replied, "Three polar
bears and two seal." If these varieties were to
be all we should find on Wrangell Island, we
should still be able to sustain life, if only we could
get enough of them. I should have liked, however,
to know that caribou and reindeer, too, could be
had for the shooting.

We now made a snow shelter and started in on
the fourteenth to dry out our boots and stockings;
we had plenty of firewood. Keruk looked after
this work. Maurer's and Malloch's feet still
troubled them and Mamen's knee was a constant
cause of suffering, so that I was glad that they
could now have an opportunity to rest. From the
moment of our departure from Shipwreck Camp
we had been constantly on the move during every
minute of the daylight. The weather, though cold,
had been exceptionally fine and clear; in fact we

had not lost an hour on account of bad weather and
had been inconvenienced for only one night by
open water. As a consequence all hands were in
need of a little rest. The dogs, too, were in a reduced condition, for though they had had plenty to
eat they had worked very hard and I wanted them
to get what rest they could.

For the plan I had been evolving to make my
way across Long Strait from Wrangell Island to
the coast of Siberia and seeking an opportunity of
getting help for the party here on the island was
now about to be put to the test. We were on land
but were a long way from civilization; we need not
drown but we might starve or freeze to death if we
could not get help within a reasonable time. With
the decline of the whaling industry there was no
chance that any ship would come so far out from
the mainland so that the only way to expect help to
reach the party was to go after it. I would take
only Kataktovick with me. He was sufficiently
experienced in ice travel and inured to the hardships of life in the Arctic to know how to take care
of himself in the constantly recurring emergencies
that menace the traveller on the ever-shifting surface of the sea-ice. On my trips with Peary I had
had plenty of leads of open water to negotiate at
this time of year but that was twelve or fifteen
degrees north of where we now were. The later

the season grew the greater became the danger of the ice breaking up and making our escape from Wrangell Island possible only through the almost miraculous appearance of a chance ship, which was unlikely so far away from the coast where the trading was carried on. From now on the leads would be opening with greater and greater frequency. It behooved me to travel light and fast and get across before the southerly winds should come and set the ice moving. To attempt to get such a large number as the entire party over to Siberia at the speed that was absolutely necessary for crossing before the ice broke up was obviously out of the question. The journey from Shipwreck Camp to Wrangell Island had already been a nerve-racking experience for us all and the trip to Siberia would in many respects be harder and more dangerous than the road we had already traversed.

The great essential was time. I must make all speed to the mainland and then along the coast to East Cape, to get transportation across to Alaska, where I could send word to the Canadian Government. We had now been out of touch with civilization for months. We had brought food enough with us to the island to last the men eighty days, full rations; this would take them into June and the caches along the trail from Shipwreck Camp could be drawn on while the ice was suitable for travel. By June the birds would be back again, and always the polar bear and the seal were reliable sources of supply.

One curious thing about the Siberian journey which Kataktovick and I now had before us was that apart from the meagre information in the "American Coast Pilot," which was much of it based on reports many years old, I knew about as much about Siberia as I knew about Mars. I felt quite certain, however, that there were natives dwelling along the coast on whom we could if necessary depend for food for our dogs and ourselves.

The weather continued fine and clear nearly all day on the fourteenth, as it had been for so many days past, but towards night clouds began to come up from the south and I felt that some change in the weather was likely to take place. The wind began to blow and by the next morning had become a gale. We devoted the time to drying out our clothes, mending them and making what alterations might be necessary.

We had three igloos, the Munro-Hadley parties in one, Kerdrillo and his party in another and Mc-Kinlay, Mamen, Kataktovick and myself in the third. We were all busy, for we were getting a party ready to go back over the trail to Shipwreck Camp to pick up supplies. Drying out clothing, too, takes time and so does the constant mending of clothes and harness which went forward vigorously. The canvas, in which we had sewed up our pemmican tins before starting on the march, now proved its usefulness by furnishing us with the material necessary for making repairs in dog harness. Mamen dislocated his knee again, poor fellow, and I had a job getting it back in place; it was extremely painful for him.

On March 16 a howling northwest gale sprang up in the early morning, continuing all day long, with blinding snowdrift. On account of the storm, the party for Shipwreck Camp was unable to leave. The next morning, however, the wind had died down to a gentle breeze and at eight A. M. the men got away. We parted for journeys in opposite directions, for I planned to leave on the following day for Siberia and would have gone on the seventeenth only that I wanted to see the others safely off. Munro, Breddy and Williams, with sixteen dogs and one sledge, were the ones chosen for the work. They were to go out over the trail to Shipwreck Camp and sledge supplies in two trips across the big pressure ridge in to the still ice about twenty-five miles from land and thence to the shore

itself, their first load to consist chiefly of biscuit
and their second of pemmican.

After my departure Munro would be in general
charge of the men on Wrangell Island, as, in the
absence of the mate, he was by rank second in
command and was, moreover, well fitted for the
post. On seeing him off I went over my instructions to him, which I told him I would also
write out and leave with McKinlay when I got
away the next day. I had had McKinlay make an
inventory of the supplies and apportion them among
the party, each to be responsible for his own share.
There would be eighty days' full rations apiece,
even if they got no game or any further supplies
from the caches along the trail and at Shipwreck
Camp. During my absence I directed that the
party be divided into three detachments, living far
enough apart from one another to insure as wide a
hunting area as possible for each.

The next morning the weather was not altogether propitious but I felt that to delay any longer
was unwise. I went over the supplies with Mc-
Kinlay, wrote out my instructions to Munro and
told the men to keep up their courage, live peace-
fully and do the best they could. They all wrote
letters home which I took to mail in Alaska.

My letter of instructions to Munro was as follows:

SHORE CAMP, ICY SPIT, WRANGELL ISLAND,
                                March 18th, 1914.
My dear Mr. Munro:

I am leaving this morning with seven dogs, one sledge and Kataktovick to get the news of our disaster before the authorities at Ottawa.

During my absence you will be in charge.

I have already allocated supplies to the different parties. McKinley has four men, Hadley is with the Eskimo Kerdrillo which makes four people, Mr. Williamson three men and yourself three men.

McKinlay kindly made out a list for me and I will ask him to give a copy to you when you get back from your trip to Shipwreck Camp.

You will make a trip to Herald Island to search for traces of mate's party. On my way I will cover the coast as far as Rodgers Harbor.

The great thing of course is the procuring of game. In this Kerdrillo will be of great assistance. Let him have his dogs and the two others so he can cover a good deal of ground; and our own parties, scatter them around so that they will be able to hunt and while away the time. Give each party enough dogs, if you can spare them so that they can better cover the ground.

As we talked about distributing supplies that you bring back; give each one their proportional share. As it stands now there are 80 days' pemmican and oil for each person.

Please do all you can to promote good feeling in camp. You will assemble at Rodgers Harbor about the middle of July where I hope to meet you with a ship.

                        Sincerely yours,
                        R. A. BARTLETT,
                        Captain, C. G. S.

CHAPTER XIX

With our sledge loaded with supplies, which included forty-eight days' food for ourselves and thirty for the dogs, we shook hands all round and Kataktovick and I were off on our journey to the Siberian coast. McKinlay accompanied us for a short distance along the way. It was a hundred and nine miles in an air line from the southernmost point of Wrangell Island across to Siberia, but first we must go around the shore of the island, and the journey across the ice, like all ice travel, would not be, to say the least, exactly in a straight line. To have gone along the shore to the northwest and on around the western end of the island would have cut off some distance but Kerdrillo had already covered part of the coast that way and by going east and south I could look for traces of the missing parties in that direction.

Shortly after McKinlay left us, about half a mile from the camp, we were assailed by increasing blasts of the northwest wind, which swirled the drifting snow about us and prevented our seeing more than a hundred yards. We followed the

171

crest of Icy Spit to the main shore and then continued along the line of the coast. At times we could not see more than a dozen yards ahead of us and the wind kept on increasing in violence. The travelling, however, so far as the going under foot was concerned, was very good, because the snow was hard and windswept. We followed the lagoons down to Bruch Spit and then kept close alongshore, inside of the heavy grounded floes. On our way we passed quantities of stranded driftwood. At 6.30 P. M. we stopped near Skeleton Island and built our igloo for the night.

When we started to use our tea boiler, after we had finished our igloo and crawled inside, we found that in some unaccountable manner a small hole had opened in the bottom, though I had tried out this boiler the last thing before I left the camp. So I made use of a device which I had learned when I was a little boy in Newfoundland. One Saturday, I remember, we went berry-picking and took along a great iron boiler to cook our dinner in. When we came to use the boiler we found there was a crack in it so that it leaked. We had with us some hard Newfoundland biscuit and my Grandmother Bartlett soaked a couple of pounds of these biscuit, plastered them inside the boiler over the crack and made it all tight. Another time I was going up to Labrador in our steam launch. It was early in the season and we had to go through a good deal of loose ice; by and by the bow struck a piece of ice and sprang a-leak. I had about sixty-five pounds of these biscuit on board; we built a dam up in the bow and put the biscuit in it; when they got well saturated with the incoming water they made a kind of cement wall that stopped the leak and saved the day. So now when I found that our tea-boiler was leaking, I remembered these boyhood experiences, and chewing up a small piece of the ship's biscuit which we had with us I plastered it over the bottom of the boiler and we were able to use it without further difficulty.

At the first crack of dawn the next morning, we broke camp, had our breakfast and started on our way again. The wind was still blowing a gale from the northwest and the snow drifted around us, as it had the day before. We followed along the shore, keeping a sharp lookout for traces of the lost parties. Little or no driftwood was to be seen along here; in fact, high cliffs came down to the water's edge and left no beach for driftwood to lodge. At 11 A. M. we passed Hooper Cairn, which was built by a party from the U. S. Revenue-cutter *Corwin* in August, 1881. The cairn, as I could see, was still intact, though I did not go up on the edge of the cliff to examine it. The only animal life that we saw all day was a raven and a lemming; we saw no bear tracks, old or new. As we went along under the high cliffs the wind at times would come sweeping down a gorge in terrific squalls that almost lifted us off our feet and whirled the snow down from the mountain-sides in huge drifts. This cloud of snow, constantly enveloping the island, was the thing that had prevented us from seeing it on our way in from Shipwreck Camp, until we were comparatively close to it. With the snow came myriad particles of sand and pieces of soft shale from the face of the cliff that cut like a knife. The dogs were pulling fairly well and we had no difficulty in getting along. At half past five we built our igloo and turned in.

When we started again at dawn on the twentieth the northwest gale and the blinding snowdrift were still with us. We had camped only a few miles from Rodgers Harbor and after crossing the spit which forms the south side of the harbor we went on over the ice in the harbor and followed the shore around to find out definitely whether any one had made a landing there. There were no traces of man to be seen.

It had been my intention to go as directly as possible from Rodgers Harbor across Long Strait to Cape North on the Siberian coast, but when we got out on the ice I found that on account of the

fact that the water here was deep near the shore
great pieces of ice had been pressed in, with high
rafters, between which were masses of soft, deep
snow. We spent some time trying to find a way
through and to make a road for the sledge to travel
over but finally decided that too many hours would
thus be consumed and kept on to the westward,
still following the shore-line. That night, with the
darkness upon us, we built our igloo about a mile
to the westward of Hunt Point. We had been on
the march since early morning, but had accomplished
little, excepting to find out that we should be unable to make a trail out over the ice at this point.

We broke camp the next day at early dawn.
The wind was now coming from the east and the
drifting snow whirled about us in clouds. Along
here it was a toss-up whether it would be better to
go along the sea-ice or travel on the land; the ice
was piled in on the shore and so badly raftered that
we had to use the pickaxe constantly, besides being
drifted deep with soft snow, in which the dogs and
sledge made heavy going and we ourselves on our
snowshoes had much ado to pick our way along,
and yet when we tried the land we found that the
wind had blown the rocks bare of snow, which made
hard going for the sledge. The dogs were not
working so well, and when we made our igloo at
dark we had finished a day's hard work that had

had many discouraging features about it. We had
been compelled to go as carefully as possible to
conserve our energy and yet, work as we might,
we did not seem to be getting any nearer a point
of departure for Siberia, and of course the farther
west we now went along the southern shore of
Wrangell Island the longer would be our eastward
journey when once we reached the mainland.

Consequently, after we took up our journey the
next morning we made another effort to find a way
out through the rafters and the deep snow. About
noon we had to abandon the attempt and turn back
to the land; on the way back we broke one of the
runners of the sledge and had to stop for about
two hours to repair it. When we finally reached
the land again we found better going, after we had
followed the shoreline westward for a little while,
and as we approached the mouth of Selfridge Bay
we found it improving more and more. We got
out on the ice along shore and found the way easier
than it had been before, so that we were able to get
to Blossom Point before we camped. The sky
was overcast all day and the light was very bad.
While Kataktovick was building the igloo at night
I went on ahead for some distance and found that
the going was getting still better.

The next morning we started out over the ice.
Shortly after we left our camp we broke our sledge

again but Kataktovick soon had it repaired.
While he was working on it, I went ahead with the
pickaxe. We got under way again and worked
through the raftered ice all day long, making the
road much of the way. Ahead of us, beyond the
edge of the raftered ice, we could see that the air
was filled with condensation, indicating the presence
of open water and showing that the ice outside the
raftered ice must be moving under the impetus of
the high, westerly wind. Just before dark we almost reached the edge of the still ice, about five
miles from land. Here we found a very high
rafter which, though not very wide, would nevertheless retard us for two hours while we completed
the road. Once we were out on the running ice,
as we should be by the next day, we should have
much easier going, though we should undoubtedly
have a great deal of open water to contend with.
We made our igloo on the raftered ice. I was
wearing snow-goggles and though I slept in them,
so that I could get my eyes well accustomed to
them, my left eye was now paining me a good deal.
From the time we left Blossom Point I never again
in our journey got a sight of Wrangell Island, on
account of the overcast sky and the drifting snow.

On March 24 we started at dawn as usual and
were not long in working our way through the
rough going in the rafter out upon the running ice.

CHAPTER XX

From now on, our journey became a never-ending series of struggles to get around or across lanes of open water—leads, as they are called,—the most exasperating and treacherous of all Arctic travelling. We would come to a lead and, leaving the sledge and dogs by it, Kataktovick would go in one direction and I in the other; when either of us found a place where we could cross he would fire a revolver or, if the whirling snow and the condensation were not too thick would climb up on some rafter where he could be seen by the other and make a signal to come on. Sometimes there would be a point where the ice on the opposite sides of the lead almost met and by throwing the dogs over, bridging the sledge across and jumping ourselves, we could manage to reach the opposite edge of the ice; at other times the lead would be too wide for this method and we would have to look for a floating ice-cake or a projecting piece that we could break off to use as a ferry-boat. Often we would get across one difficult lead—and they all had their peculiar difficulties—and then in almost no time would find ourselves confronted by another. We consumed a great deal of time crossing the leads and even more in finding a place to cross, for sometimes, no matter how far we looked in either direction—and it was not safe for us to get too widely separated—we would find that in the middle of a lead there was a narrow platform of thin ice, not strong enough to bear the sledge. It called for the exercise of all the training I had gained in my twenty years of Newfoundland sealing and Arctic exploration with Peary to negotiate these constantly recurring leads with any degree of safety.

We did not turn in until ten o'clock that night, for tired as we were from our first day's wrestle with the leads, we had to sit up and mend our clothes, which had been torn by the jagged rafters.

The next morning we were up and away at dawn, in a howling gale from the west and blinding snowdrift. Open water and young ice across our path sent us off at right angles to our true course. Several times during the day the sledge broke through the young ice and before we could whip up the dogs to rush across we got some of our sleeping gear wet. The dogs were badly frightened and huddled together in their terror and of course immensely increasing the danger of breaking through the ice. We saw a number of bear-tracks during the day. Somewhere along the trail we lost

McKinlay   Williamson   Templeman   Chafe   Williams

FIVE OF THE MEN OF THE *KARLUK* ON WRANGELL ISLAND

the little hatchet which we had for opening pemmican tins. When we missed it, we left the dogs, thinking that it might have been dropped only a short distance away, and walked back to look for it, but we found the ice changing materially and were afraid to go far from our sledge, so we had to abandon the search, and thereafter had to use a knife in its place. At half past five, when we stopped and built our igloo, a job that always took about three quarters of an hour at the end of our day's march, we had advanced during the day not over four miles. At this rate the journey from shore to shore would be a long one. The wind was moderating somewhat, however, when we turned in, and we hoped for better weather next day.

Sure enough when we broke camp the following morning we found the wind a light easterly and the weather fine. It looked as if good going must now be in store for us; we had had almost continuously stormy weather from the moment of our departure from Icy Spit. Another encouraging thing was that shortly after we started on our way, we shot a seal in a wide lead of water. The Eskimo used a native device for retrieving the seal. This device consists of a wooden ball, as large as a man's fist, made something like a stocking darner, with hooks projecting from it on all sides; there is a handle eight or ten inches long, with a white cotton fishing line attached to it about fifty fathoms long. The Eskimo would whirl this ball around and around by the handle, sometimes first putting lumps of ice on the slack line near the handle to add to the weight and thus increase the momentum, and would then let it fly out beyond where the body of the seal was floating. By carefully drawing in the line he would hook the seal and pull it along to the edge of the ice. On this occasion Kataktovick had to lie down and worm his way out on thin ice to get near enough to the water's edge to make his cast, which he made when he found a piece of heavier ice on which he could stand. I had him fastened to me by a rope, so that when he finally hooked the seal, he hauled it in hand over hand to the place where he was standing and then, while he kept his feet firmly together and slid, I hauled him back on to the solid ice where I was, while he in turn was towing the seal.

Our hope of better weather proved to be short-lived, for as the day wore on the wind increased to a living gale from the east. The ice was constantly in motion and we had many wide leads to negotiate. With the open water the air was filled with condensation and the light was very bad. When it came time to build our igloo we had made only about five miles to the good.

Shortly after midnight the wind veered sharply

around until it blew from the west, without diminishing. We had a small tent with us and to save time we were in the habit of using this as the roof for our igloo, weighting it down with snow-blocks and a rifle, pemmican tins and snowshoes, and covering the whole with snow to make it tight. When the wind changed it whipped off this canvas roof and the first thing we knew we were covered with snow. We turned out in the darkness and looked for our things which were almost completely buried.

It was not a restful night and when daylight came we were glad to be on the march again. Shortly after we started one of the dogs broke his trace and got away. Fortunately we caught him before he had gone far. Some of the dogs were docile and when we unharnessed them would not stray away but would let us harness them up again when the time came; others would try to evade us and we had to coax them in with pemmican before we could catch them.

Being so often adrift on running ice, as we were, is really a wild experience that is hard on dogs and ours were so tired that with two exceptions they did not work well. When we came to open water it took a great deal of urging to get them to jump across; often we had to unharness them and throw them across, one after another. I had a bamboo

pole, split at one end; I would shake this over the
dogs when we were on the march and the rattling
of the loose ends would serve as a stimulus for them
to buckle down to work.

On one occasion the whole team broke away from
sledge and started back over the trail. I was very
much afraid that they might run all the way back
to Wrangell Island, leaving us with the sledge
half way to Siberia, so I took a pemmican tin and
went through all the motions of opening it to feed
them and then started to walk back towards them.
I dared not run after them, for the more I ran the
faster they would go. After I had walked back half
a mile I got near enough to attract their attention.
They pricked up their ears, looked around, saw
the tins of pemmican and finally came back slowly
towards me. When they got near enough I seized
the rope. They evidently were afraid they were
in for a licking, for they stayed on their good be-
havior for several hours.

One great trouble that we had with them was
their habit of chewing their harness, though it was
made of hemp canvas instead of sealskin to prevent that very thing. In the night they would
free themselves in this way and we would have
difficulty in catching them, for although they had
collars we had no chains left. Food, clothing and
sledge-lashings had to be kept away from the dogs

or they would chew any of them. One of the dogs was called Kaiser. He got away one morning and I could not catch him, even though I tried to tempt him with pemmican. We harnessed up the others and started on our way. All day he came along behind us, sometimes in sight, sometimes not. When we stopped to camp and I fed the other dogs, at dark, he finally came sulkily in and hung around; I paid no attention to him. I saved out his ration of pemmican, however, and when he finally could hold out no longer, he came up to be fed and as I gave him the pemmican I caught him. He never got away again; sometimes we had to tie his mouth so that he could not chew his harness.

At ten o'clock on the morning after our miserable midnight hunt in the snow, we were stopped by an open lead of water about three hundred yards wide. The lead ran east and west across our way and we had to follow along the northern edge for some distance before we found a solid piece of ice for our ferry-boat. It was frozen to the edge of the main floe by thin ice, but we chopped away with our tent poles and jumped on it until we split it off. Then we put the dogs and the sledge aboard and with our snowshoes for paddles made our way across the lead. The ice cake was about ten feet square and one end of the sledge projected out over the water, but with the dogs huddled in the middle and ourselves paddling on either side we managed to get along and landed safely on the other shore.

About five we stopped to camp for the night. I was engaged in brushing the snow off the sleeping-robes and Kataktovick was cutting out snow-blocks for the igloo when suddenly he shouted. I looked up and saw right beside us the largest polar bear I have ever seen. I seized the rifle and fired. The first shot missed but the second hit him in the fore-shoulder and the third in the hind-quarter and down he went. As he fell he stretched out his four paws and I had a chance to get a good idea of his length; I should judge that he was twelve or thirteen feet from tip to tip. His hair was snow white and very long but not very thick; evidently he was old. I cut off a hind-quarter—all we could carry—to take along with us the next day; we ate some of the meat—raw, because we had no time to cook it—and made a broth out of another piece by boiling it in water, made by melting the snow, just as we made our tea. We gave the dogs all they could eat. They had not noticed the bear; they were too tired. Evidently he had come upon the place where we had cut up the seal we had killed the day before and had followed the scent all day.

Not long after I shot the bear I saw a white
Arctic fox near by.   At first I thought he was one
of the dogs.   I fired at him, but it was too dark to
see to hit him and he got away.   He, too, had evidently been attracted by the pieces of raw seal meat,
which we had scattered around when we had eaten it
earlier in the day, and had followed us.   The dogs
took no more notice of the fox than they had of
the bear.

The next day the strong east wind continued.
The sky was overcast and as there was much snowdrift the light was bad; we were shaping our course
altogether by the compass.   The temperature, I
should guess, was about fifteen degrees below zero.
We broke camp at seven o'clock and had not gone
more than fifty yards when we found that during
the night an open lead had made in the ice.   We
followed our usual method of procedure in such a
case, Kataktovick going in one direction and I in
the other, to find a better place to cross.   We had
no luck and returned to meet again at the sledge.
We now made up our minds to try to cross here.
There was a good deal of young ice in the lead,
that had been smashed up against the edges of the
heavier ice, and the snow that had been blown off
the ice into the water had filled up the lead to some
extent and ice and snow had all frozen together in a
rough and irregular mass.   I took two tent-poles,

therefore, and got out on this young ice but I soon
realized that it was not strong enough to hold me,
so I hastily and carefully made my way back.
Kataktovick, however, was lighter than I; he laid
the poles on the ice and, with a rope fastened to him
so that I could pull him back if he broke through,
he crawled over on the young ice and reached the
other side in safety.   Then I unloaded the sledge
and fastened another rope to it at the stern; Kataktovick drew it across with just a few articles on it
and I pulled it back empty.   We repeated this
until we got everything on the farther side of the
lead.   The dogs got across by themselves, all but
Kaiser; I could take no chances with him, on account of his propensity for running away, so he
had to be tied and hauled across.   I got over by
lying face downward on the empty sledge and
having Kataktovick, with the rope over his shoulder,
run as fast as he could and pull me across.   The
ice, which was only a single night's freezing, buckled
and the runners broke through in places but Kataktovick got going so fast that they did not break
through their full length and I got over in safety.
Kataktovick's safe passage was a relief to me.   As
far as physical endurance went I think he was as
well able to survive a fall in the water as I would
have been but his experience had been less than
mine and if he had fallen through he would have

been so completely terrified that I believe he would have died of fright.

The method by which he worked his way across with the poles was one which is followed among the Newfoundland sealers; many a time I had done the same thing when I was a youngster. You take bigger chances in sealing than we averaged to take in the Arctic. You leave the ship in the morning and go out on the ice to kill seals. You take no tea, no tent or shelter of any kind; perhaps all you have is a little food in your bag. The weather is fine and offers no indications of change. You get off eight or ten miles from the ship, which is perhaps the only one in that vicinity, a couple of hundred miles from land, when suddenly the ice cracks and open leads form between you and the ship. Your only chance of safety is that the men on the ship, who are constantly sweeping the horizon with powerful glasses, have foreseen what is going to happen and know where you are. If the ice is open near the ship they will steam over and pick you up. If not they will blow the whistle and let you know where the ship is, for the chances are that there is a storm breaking upon you with high winds and snow, so that you can see the ship only a short time. You have no dogs, no canvas, no snowshoes, no hot coffee, no stove. If the ship cannot reach you, or you cannot make your way across the leads and reach her, you freeze to death. I remember getting into a situation like this when I was a boy; fortunately I was rescued before things got too bad.

When we got our sledge, dogs, supplies and ourselves across the lead we had to load up again. The wind was still blowing hard and whirling the snow around, so that we lost a good deal of time hunting for things in the drifts and loading the sledge again. It was a slow job. Everything was white; boxes, bags, sleeping-robes, all the objects of our search, in fact, were blended into the one dead tone, so that the effect on the eye was as if one were walking in the dark instead of what passed technically for daylight. The drifts all looked level but the first thing we would know we would stumble into a gulch of raftered ice, heaped full of soft snow, or a crack in the ice, covered by a similar deceptive mass. Altogether we lost three hours and not until ten o'clock did we get under way again.

When we finally started we soon found the weather better. This was fortunate, for in crossing the lead and afterwards in picking up our things, we had got our clothes and our sleeping-robes more or less water-soaked and we were glad of a more moderate gale and a higher temperature, which as the afternoon wore on became almost springlike. This would mean open water, to be sure, but for the rest of the day we went along well over old floes of heavy ice where the going was good and the open leads few. About noon it came off clear and calm, and during the afternoon we made good progress. In fact, when, just at dark, we stopped and built our igloo, we had done the best day's work since we had left the island.

For the first time, too, we built our igloo on a solid floe where we could sleep without the constant menace of a split in the ice beneath us during the night. We found a floe of fresh-water ice near by; up to this time we had found few of these, none at our stopping-places, and had had to use snow to make our tea. The dogs had worked well all day; it was a relief to go on for hour after hour without having to stop for open water.

The next morning, when we were still in our igloo, finishing our tea, we heard the dogs outside, sniffing and whining excitedly; something was up. We always kept our rifle in the igloo when we made camp, with the magazine full. Now, jabbing a hole in the side of the igloo, we looked out; the dogs were moving about restlessly. Kataktovick seized the rifle and jumped outside, with me close at his heels. A bear was just making off; he had evidently come close and had been frightened by the dogs. Kataktovick ran after him and fired

twice, the first shot hitting the bear in the hind-
quarter, the second in the foreshoulder, bringing
him down.   Before I had our things out of the
igloo and loaded on the sledge, he came back,
bringing in a hindquarter of bear-meat with him.
We fed some to the dogs, though not too much,
for if we let them overeat they would not work well.
Some of it we took with us; we could not carry
much, however.

At seven o'clock we finally got away but were
soon held up by a lead of open water which in some
places was half a mile wide.   Looking from a high
rafter we could see no chance to cross in either direction, east or west, so we took up our march eastward, the course of the lead gradually veering to
the southeast.

As we went along we saw several seal in the
water.   One of these we shot and recovered after
some difficulty.   The Eskimo captured the seal in
the usual way and towed it to the edge of the ice,
which at this point was about five feet above the
surface of the water.   As the seal came alongside,
I reached down to haul it up.   Braced against a
hummock, Kataktovick held my feet to keep me
from sliding down into the water and I caught
hold of the seal by the flipper and held it.   The
seal was not quite dead and made some resistance.
On account of my position I could get no pur-

chase on the ice to pull up with my arms and the
seal weighed about a hundred pounds. I managed
to lift it out of the water far enough to get its hind
flipper in my teeth, and then Kataktovick hauled
us back. When I got up a little way he passed
me a rope and I jabbed a hole in the flipper and
passed the rope through. I was then able to let go
with my teeth, sprang up with the rope in my hand
and dragged the seal up on to the level ice. We
skinned it and cut it up and put as much of the
meat on the sledge as we could carry, giving the
dogs a very little. We could have got more seal
here but one was all we could take. Our food
consisted very largely of frozen bear meat and seal
meat now, eaten raw because we had no time to
cook it. This saved our pemmican.

About noon we ferried over the lead and found
the going so good on the other side that when,
travelling as long as possible to make the most of
it, we built our igloo after dark, we had made at
least nine miles south of the point where we started
our day's march, though the long tramp along the
lead had made our total distance travelled considerably more than that.

CHAPTER XXI

March 30—the thirteenth day of our journey from Icy Spit—was the first fine day we had had. We broke camp at dawn. Almost at once we encountered open water and from that time until dark crossed lead after lead. One of them was half a mile wide. It was filled with heavy pieces of ice, frozen into precarious young ice, the whole mass only solid enough to enable us to get a few things at a time over on the sledge. We had to unharness our dogs and haul the lightly loaded sledge across, picking our way from one heavy piece to another as a man zigzags his way across a creek on stepping-stones. It took a good many trips to get everything over.

The sunset was clear and all around the horizon there was not a cloud in the sky. Looking to the southwest I saw what I was inclined to believe was land. Perhaps the wish might be father to the thought, and the days of travel over the white surface of the ice, with the constant effort to find a place to cross the innumerable leads had brought

my eyes to a state of such acute pain that I could
not see as well as usual.   I turned my binoculars
on the cloudlike mass on the horizon but still I remained in doubt.

So I called to the Eskimo and, pointing, asked
him, "That land?"

He answered that it might be.

Then I gave him the glasses and sent him up on
a high rafter to look more carefully.   After a moment he came back and said that it might be an
island like Wrangell Island but that it would be
of no use to us.   He seemed depressed by the hard
day we had had, crossing so many leads.   Finally
he turned to me and said:

"We see no land, we no get to land; my mother,
my father, tell me long time ago Eskimo get out
on ice and drive away from Point Barrow never
come back."

I tried to hearten him by telling him that Eskimo
out on the ice did not have to get back by themselves but that the white men would bring them
back and that I had been a long distance out on the
ice with Eskimo and we had all got back safely.
He still seemed pretty much discouraged, so I took
the glasses and went up on the rafter to see for
myself, though his eyes were in a better condition
than mine.   I made every effort to see as well as
I could and was convinced that I was looking at

the land. When I called Kataktovick up to look again he was still very dubious.

That night in our igloo when we were making our tea, he asked me to show him the chart. I did so and pointed out the course we had taken and where we were bound. He appeared somewhat encouraged, though still of the opinion that the land was not Siberia but merely an island, not set down on the chart. When I tried to brace him up, however, by saying, "If you 'fraid, you no reach land," he did not respond very enthusiastically and slept less soundly than usual that night.

The next day dawned fine and clear. We got out of our igloo before sunrise, when the horizon was bright and objects along the surface of the ice were sharply defined against the skyline; sunrise and sunset are the best times to see anything at a distance. A good night's sleep had rested my eyes and when I looked through my binoculars from the top of the ridge I could see the land distinctly, covered with snow. I was surprised to be able to see it so clearly. I called to Kataktovick to come up.

"Me see him, me see him *noona* (land)," he said; he had been up on the rafter, he added, before I had got out of the igloo.

" What you think him?" I asked. "You think him all right?"

"Might be, might be, perhaps," he replied.

Evidently he was still dubious about its being Siberia. He had been satisfied by the chart the night before; at Shipwreck Camp and again at Wrangell Island I had explained the charts to him, had shown him where we were going, what we were going to do with the charts, how far away Siberia was and how far we should have to travel to meet Eskimo, expressing the distances by comparing them with the distance from Point Barrow to the deer camp, for instance, or down to Cape Lisburne, trips that were familiar to him. Now, however, he still appeared skeptical of the identity of the land we were looking at. He said it was not Siberia. When I asked why, he replied that he had been told by his people that Siberia was low land. I explained to him that the shore was, it was true, low in many places, running out for miles into the sea. This low fore-shore was known as the tundra; owing to the distance we could see only the hinterland behind it, which was high. Kataktovick listened to my explanation and then shook his head. It might be an island, he said; Alaskan Eskimo on the Siberian shore, so he had been told, are always set upon and killed by the Eskimo there. I told him as best I could that the Siberian Eskimo were just as kindly disposed towards wayfarers as the Alaskan Eskimo and that he had nothing to fear.

I think he still rather hoped that the land we saw was not Siberia but a new island, so that he might postpone as long as possible the horrible fate he was convinced was in store for him.

From the time we started that morning we had leads of water and treacherous young ice to contend with. In some places we could get across easily; in others we had to make wide detours. At noon we stopped on the north side of a narrow lead and Kataktovick made a little snow igloo to serve as shelter while we rested for awhile. He understood perfectly how to use the Primus stove and he made some tea. While he was doing this I reconnoitered to the eastward, walking probably two miles before I came to a point where we could cross. When I returned to the sledge the Eskimo had the tea ready and we found it most refreshing. We could always eat bear meat whenever we were hungry. It got frozen on the sledge, of course, but with a knife or a hatchet we would chip off small pieces, or sometimes we would thaw it out by rolling it up in our shirts and letting our bodily heat melt the frost.

We now went on to the eastward to the point I had selected for crossing the lead. There was young ice here but it was not very strong, so we had to adopt our customary expedient of pulling the sledge over and back lightly loaded. Once across we went on for some time without trouble with open water but presently found ourselves among heavy raftered ice, with high pinnacles and in between them masses of snow, deep and not very hard. We had to use the pickaxe a good deal and the dogs had hard going. Three of them were getting to be very sick.

Towards the end of the day we could see the land distinctly, about forty miles away. When we built our igloo at dark we had made at least ten miles to the good, though our actual march had been longer than that. The Eskimo appeared very much depressed. I was naturally feeling cheerful myself because in two or three days we should be on land. Furthermore I believed most of our troubles with open leads would soon be over, as we approached nearer the shore ice, though the going would probably be rough from the pressure of the running-ice on the still ice, just as we had found it in getting away from Wrangell Island.

During the latter part of our day's journey I fell and hurt my side. My eyes troubled me more than ever, because I broke the glass in my goggles and, though I had another pair, I did not find that they suited me as well as those to which I had become accustomed. Kataktovick, too, wore goggles.

On April 1 we made a good day's march. The going was rather rough, but we were fortunate in finding the young ice firm enough to bear us so that we did not lose much time in getting across the leads to the big floes where it was smoother and more level. About three o'clock in the afternoon we came to a belt of raftered ice and deep, soft snow, where we had to use the pickaxe. After two hours' work we got through and had good going the remainder of the day.

We got away from our igloo at six o'clock the next morning and found that the going continued good for a while. After a time we came to another patch of rough, heavy ice, with open leads, which we had to cross. Then we came to a long strip of firm, young ice and had good travelling, later reaching older floes and raftered ice; we managed to make our way round the ends of the rafters and did not have to use the pickaxe at all. This was a great relief for we wasted no time in making a road. The dogs, however, were pretty nearly worn out and could only be made to work by constant urging; in fact, during the day two of them gave out completely.

We made camp at half past seven. The land was not over fifteen or eighteen miles away, so we knew that we had done a good day's work.

At about one o'clock the next morning, while we were asleep, the ice split near the igloo and opened about two feet. We had to get out of the igloo at once because, although the crack did not come inside, it was so near that the walls split on the south end. Shortly after we got out the ice began to move about and we had to work fast to save the dogs. Some of them had been tethered and others loose; now we let them all loose to give each a better opportunity if the ice broke up any more, taking our chances on getting them together again in the morning. We removed everything from the igloo and loaded up the sledge, lashing everything tight. The night was fine and clear, with brilliant starlight and no wind whatever, all of which was in our favor, though it was still so dark that we could not see our way around.

We stayed up the rest of the night and at dawn had some meat and pemmican and drank some tea. As soon as it was light enough we got away, hoping that by night we should be on land. The ice was in motion everywhere, however, and there were open leads on every hand. We had light enough to see what we had to do but there was a great deal of condensation and we could not see very far. The ice was grinding and groaning, and splitting in all directions about us as we travelled and the noise made the dogs so uneasy that at times they were practically useless. Finally, about three o'clock in the afternoon, the light was so bad and the ice was moving so constantly that we could not get along so we stopped, built our igloo, drank some tea and turned in.

At six o'clock the next morning, the fourth of April, we left the dogs and the sledge in camp and went ahead with pickaxes to make a trail through the rough ice. It was a fine, clear day. From a high rafter I could see an open lead on the other side of the belt of rough ice, and beyond the lead the ice-foot, itself, as it is called in Arctic parlance, —the ice which is permanently attached to the land and extends out into the sea.

At ten o'clock, leaving Kataktovick to continue the road-making with the pickaxe, I went back to the camp, harnessed up the dogs and drove them along the trail that we had made. When we reached the open lead we had to look for a place to cross. Finally we found a point where the moving ice nearly touched the still ice. The dogs, however, were so frightened that they were afraid to stir. We tried to make them jump across the crack but they lay down and would not budge. While we delayed thus the crack widened; the moving floe was drifting away. I made up my mind that it was now or never, so I cut the traces, jumped across the widening gap and pulled the sledge across. Then I threw a rope to Kataktovick and pulled him across flying. The dogs we managed to grasp by traces or wherever we could get hold of them and dragged them across. Before long the lead had opened to a considerable width. We were now on the land ice, free from open water, and had only rafters, rough ice and deep snow to contend with. I sent Kataktovick on towards the land to see how the going was and I started in to make a road with the pickaxe, while the dogs rested by the sledge. In about an hour he came back and said that after he had got through the rough ice he had found the going good. We both worked on the road with our pickaxes and in the afternoon got about through the rough ice to smoother going beyond. I went back and brought up the dogs and the sledge and by the time I reached Kataktovick he was through the rough ice. It was a fine, clear day, without any wind; the temperature, I should judge, was about fifty below zero.

The good going did not last long for we soon came to rough ice, with deep, soft snow. Here we had to wear our snowshoes again. For a good part of the way across from Wrangell Island we had not been able to use them because the ice was too rough and jagged and, furthermore, we had had so much jumping to do, getting across the leads, that we could not spare the time necessary to put the snowshoes on and off, or run the risk of breaking them. Our footgear was wet, too, and the ugsug rawhide straps across the toes sank in so far that there was danger that our feet would freeze by the stopping of the circulation. Yet, wherever it is practicable to wear them, snowshoes are indispensable in Arctic travel and I should as willingly do without food as without snowshoes. At this point we threw all the supplies off the sledge excepting enough for one day and, with the sledge light, made the road with pickaxes towards the land.

The Eskimo now showed by his manner that he was feeling more optimistic. Finally, as we were working our way through the rough ice, he said that he smelled wood-smoke, and asked whether I smelled it, too. I did not but I had no doubt that he did, for an Eskimo's sense of smell is remarkably acute. I felt sure that we were not far from human habitation, though just what this might be I could only guess. From the leaves of the "American Coast Pilot" that I had with me, I was able to learn that "the northeast coast of Siberia has been only slightly examined, and the charts must be taken as sketches and only approximately accurate. The first examination was by Cook, in 1778; the next exploration was by Admiral von Wrangell in 1820; in 1878, Baron Nordenskiöld, in the *Vega,* passed along the coast, having completed the N. E. passage as far as Pitlekaj, where he was frozen in and wintered. In 1881 the coast was examined

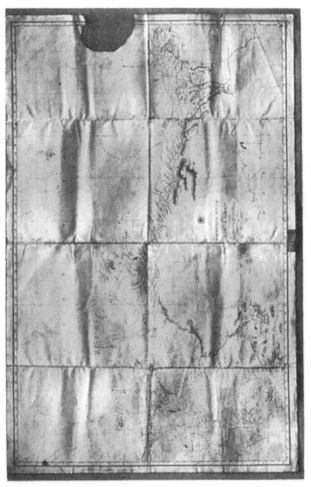

CAPTAIN BARTLETT'S CHART OF THE ALASKAN COAST FROM THE
MACKENZIE RIVER TO BERING STRAIT

in places by Lieut. Hooper of the U. S. S. *Corwin,*
and the description of the salient points here given
is from the report of the *Corwin.*" This was not
exactly what could be called up-to-date information. In the *Karluk's* library had been a copy of
Nordenskiöld's "Voyage of the *Vega,*" but it was
in German, a language which I am unable to read.
The pictures indicated that woods extended in
places down to the shore and that reindeer lived in
the woods. What I particularly wanted to know,
however, was in what condition the Siberian natives
now were, what food they had to eat, and whether
they were afflicted with tuberculosis, to which so
many primitive races have succumbed after contact
with the beneficent influences of civilization, for
more than thirty years had elapsed since Nordenskiöld's journey and in that length of time radical
changes in numbers or habitation might have come
to the whole population.

Late in the afternoon we got through the rough
ice and for the remaining mile or so to the shore
had good going. At five o'clock in the afternoon
we landed on the Siberian coast. It was the fourth
of April and we had been seventeen days on the
march. The distance we had actually gone in making the journey was not less than two hundred
miles.

The first thing the Eskimo saw when we reached the land was the trail of a single sledge along the tundra.

"*Ardegar* (that's good)," he said; "Eskimo come here."

I asked him if it was Siberia and he said it was.

"Where we go?" I asked.

Without a moment's hesitation he pointed to the east.

A snowstorm had already begun, while we were still on the march, and it was now coming on with rapidly increasing violence, so we set to work at once and in half an hour had an igloo built, and a shelter for our dogs, now reduced to four. When we got inside the igloo we made tea, boiled some of the bear meat we had with us and ate until we could eat no more. Then we turned in. It seemed pretty good to sleep on land again.

CHAPTER XXII

WE MEET THE CHUKCHES

At dawn the next morning we left our igloo and went back over the trail we had made to the place where we had thrown off our supplies the afternoon before. Owing to the bad light and the drifting snow, we had a good deal of trouble in picking up our things and the trail itself was frequently obscured, but we managed to get our stuff together again and by nine o'clock were back at our igloo ready to begin our march eastward. We made some tea and at ten o'clock started on our way. On account of the overcast sky and the thick snow we could see little of the surrounding country and I had no way of telling just where we were. Later on, when I had a chance to go over the chart with Baron Kleist at East Cape, I figured out that we had landed near Cape Jakan, about sixty miles west of Cape North.

We found the travelling excellent along the tundra. The trail was plainly marked, for the wind had swept the land nearly bare of snow, and the tracks of the sledge that had passed that way before were defined enough to be easily followed. After

our days of stumbling over the rough ice and crossing open leads it seemed as simple as walking along
a country road.   Our dogs were in bad shape and
only one of the four was of any real use.

About two o'clock in the afternoon we could
make out black objects some distance ahead of us;
as we drew nearer we could see that they were moving.   Kataktovick had been ahead, while I drove
the dogs; now he stopped, came back and said,
"Eskimo igloo."

"*Ardegar,*" I replied, and told him to go on.

He set his face eastward again and I urged the
dogs harder than ever.   Ordinarily he was a good
walker but now he seemed to be lagging a little
and dropping back, nearer and nearer the dogs.
I asked him what the matter was.

"Eskimo see me, they kill me," he said.   "My
father my mother told me long time ago Eskimo
from Point Barrow go to Siberia, never come back,
Siberian Eskimo kill him."

I told him that he was mistaken and repeated
what I had said the day before about the hospitality of the Siberian Eskimo.   Our troubles were
at an end, I said; we should now have a place to
dry our clothes and get them mended, or perhaps
get new ones.   "Maybe," I added, " we get tobacco."

Kataktovick was still reluctant, even though I

told him that perhaps we could get some dogs, or even persuade some of the Eskimo to travel along with us.

We could now make out that the objects ahead of us were human beings and that they were running about, apparently very much excited by our approach. Kataktovick hung back near the dogs. At length I said, "You drive the dogs now and I will go ahead." He did so with evident relief and so we went on until I was within ten yards of the Eskimo. Then I put out my hand and walked towards them, saying in English, "How do you do?" They immediately rushed towards us and grasped us each warmly by the hand, jabbering away in great excitement. I could understand nothing of what they were saying, nor could Kataktovick. I tried to make them understand who we were and where we had come from but they were as ignorant of my language as I was of theirs.

There could be no doubt, however, that they were glad to see us and eager to show their hospitality, for the first thing we knew they had unharnessed our dogs and were feeding them, had taken our sledge into the outer part of their house and put it, with everything still on it, up on a kind of scaffold where it would be away from the dogs and sheltered from the weather. Then an old woman caught me by the arm and pushed me into the

inner inclosure and on to a platform where three
native lamps were going, one at each end and the
other in the middle.   The roof was so low that my
head touched it, so I sat down.   The woman
brushed the snow off my clothes with a snow-beater
shaped like a sickle and thinner than ours, placed
a deerskin on the platform for me to sit on, pulled
off my boots and stockings and hung them up to
dry.   Then she gave me a pair of deerskin stockings, not so long as ours, because, as I could see,
the trousers that these Siberians wore were longer
than ours.   After that she took off my parka or
fur jacket and hung it up to dry, while I pulled
off my undershirt.   Others were waiting upon
Kataktovick in the same way and here we were,
when we had hardly had time to say, "Thank you,"
clad only in our bearskin trousers and seated comfortably about a large wooden dish, filled with
frozen reindeer meat, eating sociably with twelve
or fourteen perfect strangers to whom, it might
be said, we had not been formally introduced.
Never have I been entertained in a finer spirit of
true hospitality and never have I been more thank-
ful for the cordiality of my welcome.   It was, as I
was afterwards to learn, merely typical of the true
humanity of these simple, kindly people.

When I had time to look about me, I found that
I was seated in a large, square room, shaped some-

what like a large snow igloo, though the Siberian Eskimo or Chukches, as these natives are called, know nothing of snow igloos or how to build them. Their house, as I was presently to learn, is called an aranga. There is a framework of heavy driftwood, with a dome-shaped roof made of young saplings. Over all are stretched walrus skins, secured by ropes that pass over the roof and are fastened to heavy stones along the ground on opposite sides. The inner inclosure, which is the living apartment, is about ten feet by seven; it is separated by a curtain from the outer inclosure where sledges and equipment are kept. In the living apartment the Chukches eat and sleep on a raised platform of turf and hay, covered with tanned walrus skin. They light and heat their houses and do their cooking with a lamp which consists of a dish of walrus or seal oil, with a wick of moss in it. This is superior to wood for such a dwelling-place, for it makes no smoke; the lamp is lighted by a regulation safety match, though to be sure it is seldom allowed to go out. The three lamps in this aranga made the room pretty hot; the temperature, I should guess, was about a hundred.

Our hosts and hostesses, comprising three families who dwelt in three arangas at this place, were always drinking tea. They used copper kettles to melt the ice in and Russian tea, put up in compressed slabs a foot long, eight inches wide and three-fourths of an inch thick. In our honor the old woman brought out cups and saucers of the prettiest china I have ever seen; the cups were very small, holding about three sips. Each cup was wrapped in a dirty cloth, on which the old woman wiped it after carefully spitting on it to make it clean. When I saw her method of dish-washing, I was impolite enough to ask Kataktovick to go out and get my mug from the sledge; when he returned with it our hostess looked disappointed, though whether from the large size of the mug or because I did not apparently appreciate her kindness in using her best china for us, I cannot say.

When we had finished the wooden dish of reindeer meat, which though uncooked was good eating, they brought in another filled with walrus meat, evidently taken from a walrus killed the previous summer, which had a smell that I cannot describe. Out of politeness I tried to eat it, but found it was a little too much for me. Kataktovick enjoyed it. Later on I asked him why he wanted the same food we had aft while he was on the ship and yet was willing to eat this foul walrus meat; he said he liked it. Apparently although they live pretty much on white man's food the Eskimo enjoy getting back once in a while to walrus meat and blubber that have seen better days.

After the walrus meat we had more tea. I had about a hundred saccharine tablets with me, so when the fresh tea was brought in I used them all up in it.

I could see that the Siberians were puzzled about Kataktovick. They talked about him and to him; at first, I am quite sure, they did not think that he was an Eskimo. They evidently took me for a trader, though they had not seen me go up the coast. The sledge was all bundled up, so that they could not see what I had, and rather lightly loaded, so that apparently I had sold my goods and was now working down the coast on my homeward journey. They were in evident doubt about Kataktovick, because he and they could not understand each other's speech. He would talk to them in the language of the Alaskan Eskimo and they would put up their hands and touch their faces to show that they did not understand. Then they would talk to him and he, in turn, would throw up his hands and say, "Me no savvy."

After we had finished our second round of tea, they made signs to show that they wanted to know where we came from. I took out my charts, showed them where we drifted, pointed out Wrangell Island and told them of the men there, showed them where the ship sank and where we had just landed. I first made a ship out of matches.

When I saw that this did not convey any idea to them I drew pictures on the charts; to show where the *Karluk* sank and what happened to make her sink, I drew a picture of a ship, surrounded it with lines intended to represent ice, clapped my hands and rubbed the whole thing out. This they understood well enough to know what I was driving at. They told me their names but I could neither pronounce them nor write them. We started our feast at two o'clock and continued through the afternoon and until late at night, having tea every five minutes.

We still had four or five of the little tin boxes of tabloid tea left; there were pictures of India on the box-covers which attracted the Chukches wonderfully. I had some Burberry cloth left and I had the old woman make a bag, into which I emptied the tea; then I gave the empty tins with their pretty covers to the children. The tea tablets interested the older folk so I contributed some to the "party."

Spreading out the chart I inquired by signs about the people that we might find on our journey eastward. I was assured that we should see them all along the coast and that there were one or two communities of them like this on the way to Cape North. I could find Cape North on the chart, on which, of course, it was clearly marked. The

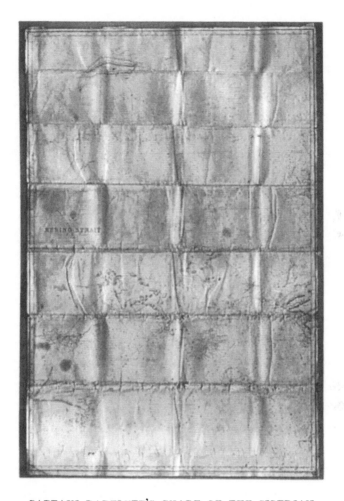

CAPTAIN BARTLETT'S CHART OF THE SIBERIAN
COAST AND BERING STRAIT

" After we had finished our second round of tea, they made signs
to show that they wanted to know where we came from.
I took out my charts, showed them where we
drifted, pointed out Wrangell Island and told
them of the men there, showed them
where the ship sank and where
we had just landed."
See page 213.

Chukches, however, did not know what I meant when I used the name but finally one of them said "Irkaipij." He repeated it again and again and at last I understood that it was another name for the same place. I laid a lot of matches on the chart, showing our course, and the same man, by means of these matches, indicated that at Cape North were several arangas. From the presence of cooking utensils, tea and tobacco I concluded, and, as I learned later, correctly, that I should run across Russian traders here and there on our march.

I wondered whether these Chukches were travellers and ever left the coast to journey into the interior of the country. By drawing pictures of trees and reindeer on the chart I found that I could make them understand what I wanted to know; then by marking on the chart they showed me that they made journeys of fifteen sleeps' duration before they reached the reindeer country. I learned afterwards that there were two kinds of natives, the coast Eskimo and the deer men, the latter a hardier type of man than the former. The coast natives get their living by hunting, their chief game being walrus, seal and bear. Some of them have large skin-boats for travelling from settlement to settlement, covering in this way considerable stretches of coast. They do not go out upon the drift ice. Two years before, so Kataktovick discovered, two hunters had got adrift on the ice and had not come back; we were now requested to tell whether we had seen any signs of them.

They establish their arangas when possible near a river, where they can fish for salmon and trout and get ice to melt for water, instead of using snow, a large quantity of which is needed for such a purpose. I found a number of men and women along the coast who were between fifty and sixty years of age, but they looked and acted older; they seem to be pretty generally affected with turberculosis, more or less developed, and do not take the right care of themselves. When they get too old and feeble to support themselves and have become a burden to others, they destroy themselves. I do not think they make any graves,—at least I saw none; apparently their bodies are left for the birds and animals to eat.

I did not, of course, acquire all my information about the natives from the first ones I met, though to be sure they were a typical group and exemplified, the more I studied them, all the customs of the country, especially that of continual feasting of the stranger within their gates.

About eleven o'clock that night we all lay down together on the bed-platform,—men, women and children; the youngsters had all remained outside the curtain until that time. The air was hot and ill-smelling, and filled with smoke from the Russian pipes which the Chukches used, pipes with little bowls and long stems, good for only a few puffs. When they were not drinking tea they were smoking Russian tobacco. All the time, with hardly a moment's cessation, they were coughing violently; tuberculosis had them in its grip. When they lay down to sleep they left the lamps burning. There was no ventilation; the coughing continued and the air was if anything worse and worse as the night wore on. Some time between two and three in the morning I woke up; I had been awake at intervals ever since turning in but now I was fully aroused. The air was indescribably bad. The lamps had gone out and when I struck a match it would not light. The Chukches were all apparently broad awake, coughing incessantly. I felt around for the curtain and when I found it held it open. This was evidently a new experience for them; they were clearly afraid of draughts. I was a guest, however, and they politely refrained from outward objections.

My diary for the next day, April 6, begins: "Anniversary of the discovery of the North Pole. No doubt in New York the Explorers' Club is entertaining Peary."

All day the wind blew hard from the northwest, with blinding snowdrifts. Had we been ever so

inclined to move we could have done little travelling
and our enforced stay gave us a good chance to
dry out our clothes, which had became saturated
with salt water and perspiration, and to mend
the numerous tears where the jagged corners of the
raftered ice had got in their work. I borrowed
boots and stockings from the natives for Kataktovick and sent him out with another Eskimo to repair our sledge, which was much the worse for wear.
We made some new dog-harness and repaired the
old. I tried to buy a dog or two here but the
natives had none to sell; in fact they had very few
dogs at any time.

Towards afternoon Kataktovick came in and
told me that he thought one of the natives would go
on to Cape North with us, taking with him his dog
and his small sledge. This was welcome news, for
by guiding us along the uncertainties of the trail
he could expedite our travelling.

I had two or three cheap watches and other
small articles and had saved half a dozen razors of
my own; these things I divided among the natives
along the way. Money, of which I had only a
little, was not much good. To the old woman who
had taken off my boots when we first arrived here
I gave a cake of soap and some needles, to her
daughter some empty tea tins and to her twelve-
year-old boy a watch and a pocket-knife. The

Siberian women are very industrious; they do all the housework, of course, sewing and mending the skin clothing, and, if need be, they drive the dogs.

With the conditions now favorable for progress along shore, I knew that, with luck, I should be able to reach civilization and arrange to have aid sent to the men on Wrangell Island. I thought about them all the time, however, and worried about them; I wondered how the storms which had so delayed our progress across Long Strait had affected Munro's chances of retrieving the supplies cached along the ice from Shipwreck Camp and getting safely back to the main party, and how the men would find life on the island as the weeks went by and they separated according to my instructions for the hunting which would sooner or later have to be their main dependence.

CHAPTER XXIII

EASTWARD ALONG THE TUNDRA

By the next morning, April 7, we were ready to start on our way. Our clothes were all dried out and in order, our sledge was repaired, our dogs were rested and the dogs and ourselves had had a chance to eat heartily and at our leisure. Before we got away an old woman from one of the other arangas came over and asked us to go to her aranga. We found that she had a lot of dried deer fat or suet, which she considered a great delicacy. She offered us some, with sugar to eat with it, and then her married daughter gave us some tea. She had about eight lumps of sugar left from her winter's stock. She made signs to ask me if I liked sugar. I said yes and took some with my tea. The way these Siberian Eskimo use their sugar is to take a sip or two of tea and then a bite of the sugar; they do not put the sugar in the tea and stir it up, but eat the sugar and wash it down with tea. The old lady also offered me a pair of deerskin mittens which were very acceptable. I gave her some needles suitable for sewing skins and she was very much pleased with them.

The morning was very bright and fine. We got away at ten o'clock with our four dogs and our sledge, and a native came along with us. He had very little on his sledge, which was small and light, and he rode a good deal. We walked as usual, not wearing our snowshoes where the snow was no deeper than it was along here. The going was pretty good. The sun was shining; there was no wind, but it was very cold. For a while our dogs kept up a good pace but they soon slowed down.

During the afternoon we passed two more arangas where we had some tea. All through the day I had the greatest difficulty in keeping my hands from being frozen; I cannot explain why. I had never had any trouble that way before but now it was only by making the most frantic efforts and keeping constantly alert that I was able to prevent their freezing. The temperature, I should guess, was between fifty and sixty below zero. We travelled along well all day and at sunset built our snow igloo. I was surprised to find that our companion knew nothing about cutting out snow blocks and that with the Siberian Eskimo building a snow igloo was evidently a lost art. On their travels from place to place along the coast they very seldom venture out unless the weather is fine, and they can always reach another aranga by the end of the day, so they have no need, I found, to build their own sleeping-place as we had been accustomed to do.

Our Eskimo had no dog food; he would get some at Cape North, he said. I still had some dog pemmican left; at his aranga he had fed our dogs so that night when I fed our dogs I gave some pemmican to his dog.

It was a great pleasure to sleep that night in our igloo. The air was not foul and close, as it had been in the aranga on the previous night, and we did not have the constant annoyance of coughing going on all around us. Our companion coughed a little when he first turned in but soon left off and we all fell asleep, not waking up until daylight.

The sky was overcast and the wind north when we broke camp at six o'clock the next morning. We could not see very far. As we proceeded along the tundra we found that it became narrower as we approached Cape North. Our Siberian companion was very kind and added his dog to the four still remaining to us. His sledge was hardly larger than a child's sled in America and we carried it easily on our sledge. By travelling hard all day we found ourselves approaching the settlement at Cape North about sunset. We had made a good two days' march in spite of the dubious weather and the extreme cold. Low temperatures were not exactly new to me but for some reason or other I felt the cold along the Siberian coast more acutely than anywhere else in all my Arctic work. There were stretches of shore line, when the wind swept unobstructed across the ice fields from the north, where I was particularly sensitive; I had no thermometer, but judging from the condition of the coal oil and comparing the general effect of the air upon my skin and its particular tendency to freeze my face and hands, I should say that the temperature was at least sixty below zero.

When we were crossing the smooth ice at the entrance to the small harbor at Cape North our guide pointed to one of the arangas on the opposite shore and made signs that we were to go there. It was nearly dark but we could see that there were eleven arangas altogether and we made our way towards the one which he pointed out. Presently we met some natives. Without hesitation they seized my arm and conducted me over to the aranga towards which we had been heading. Outside of the aranga awaiting my coming, was a very tall man, muffled up in furs. I had an idea that he was a white man so I asked, "Do you speak English?"

"Some little," he replied, and unwrapped the furs somewhat from around his face; I saw that he was a Russian.

"One man he speak more English," he added.

In a moment another Russian came along; his ability to speak English intelligibly proved to be less than the first man's. By paying careful attention to what he was saying I was able to tell approximately what he was trying to say, and thus we managed to surmount the barrier of language. I gathered that he had been a longshoreman in Seattle and that he knew that Mr. Taft had been president of the United States. He asked me, in fact, if I knew him.

While we were standing there Kataktovick came up and asked me what he should do.

"You take out the dogs," I said, "and come with me."

In the excitement at seeing a white stranger come along in this unexpected way no one thought for the moment of asking us to come into the aranga; there was no intentional inhospitality—they all simply forgot to do the honors.

After a few more attempts at conversation between the Russians and myself, a native came along and said, "You old man?"

His question puzzled me at first; presently it dawned on me that he was speaking in nautical parlance and wanted to know if I was a captain. "Yes," I replied.

"You come below in my cabin, old man," he said, meaning that I was to go into his aranga.

I followed him and we entered his aranga together. Cold as it was outside, the air inside was very warm, too warm for comfort. There were a good many people there. Talking with my host as best I could I learned that at one time he had lived at East Cape and had met some of the whalers there in the days when Arctic whaling was still a big industry; he had been aboard of them and knew their names.

"Me know *Karluk*," he said, in reply to a question of mine. "Me on board *Karluk* when she whale."

He was surprised to think that we were on a whaling voyage and I explained to him by the chart what we were trying to do and where we had been when the ship went down. He understood a good deal of what I told him and was able to understand a little of Kataktovick's language, but I could see that he was much surprised when he realized that we had walked all the way from Shipwreck Camp to get to the land. He seemed to have an idea that this was a great feat. I explained to him that Kataktovick was with me and built our igloos and killed seal and bear, and that an Eskimo and a white man could live indefinitely on the ice.

While we were talking and I was having some tea and seal meat the first of the two Russians that

we had met came in and at his invitation I went
with him back to his aranga.   Here we had a genuine meal—Russian bread, salmon, tea and milk.
I explained to him what we were doing and how the
ship was lost.   At East Cape, he said, he had a
brother who would look after us and make us comfortable; he gave me a letter of introduction to his
brother.   Their name was Caraieff.   As for himself he was bound further westward on a trading
trip to Cape Jakan.   In ten days he would be
back again at Cape North and he urged me to wait
until then; he had two fine teams of dogs that
would be of great assistance to us.   I declined his
invitation, however, for I was anxious to get on
and had an idea that after I got to East Cape I
should go to Anadyr and send my message to
Ottawa from the Russian wireless station there,
mentioned on my chart.   If I had known enough
about the Siberian coast I could have gone direct
from Cape North to Anadyr southeast across the
Chukchi Peninsula in about the time that it took
me to get from Cape North to East Cape.

I spent a very comfortable night in the aranga
occupied by Mr. Caraieff.   It was rather warm but
I shed some of my clothing and lay down on a deerskin, spread out on the bed-platform.   Mr. Caraieff and I attempted to converse before dropping
off to sleep but he spoke very little English and

I no Russian whatever, so I am afraid neither gathered much information about the other.

I have often wondered at the courteous willingness of the Russians and Chukches whom we met along our way to take entirely for granted our presence among them. They showed no impertinent curiosity and did not subject us to any unpleasant inquisition; they required no custom-house examination, no passports, no letters of recommendation! We were not traders, yet we were obviously strangers with strange travelling gear, and it was hardly likely that we were taking a walk for our health. In more than one semi-civilized country shipwrecked mariners have from the earliest times been considered fair prey for the natives. We had our charts, to be sure, but ship-wrecked mariners who go ashore driving a team of dogs are not common, even in the Arctic. Yet all the way along we were received without question, greeted hospitably, made comfortable and guided on our way with no consideration of payment; we might have been city cousins visiting around among country relatives.

Cape North, which was first seen and named by the famous English voyager, Captain Cook, in the *Resolution,* in 1778, is a point of considerable importance on the Siberian coast. Of the eleven arangas several were occupied by deer men, the men who look after herds of reindeer in the interior and come out to the coast at intervals to exchange their reindeer meat for seal and walrus meat, and for blubber for their oil lamps. Baron Kleist, whom I met later on at East Cape, told me that he had been in reindeer camps where two men owned four thousand reindeer. He had seen these men out in the open, under the necessity of look-ing after their herds constantly day and night for thirty-six hours, without shelter of any kind, and their faces, he said, were literally burned black from the frost and wind.

Before we went to sleep that night, Mr. Caraieff made tea, and as he had sugar and milk for it and some Russian bread to eat we had a very pleasant supper party. The Chukch who owned the aranga had a four-year-old grandson who ate his share of decayed walrus meat and drank his full allowance of tea with four lumps of sugar for each small cup-ful.

My eyes were affected a good deal by the irrita-tion of the overheated atmosphere, with its almost complete lack of ventilation. I found occasional relief by lifting the edge of the curtain and letting the cold air play upon my eyes. The temperature out-of-doors was about fifty below zero and bit-terly cold, much more so, Mr. Caraieff said, than we should find it nearer East Cape.

When I put my head outside of the aranga, about seven o'clock the next morning, I found that the wind was blowing almost a hurricane from the west and sweeping the snow into heavy drifts. Mr. Caraieff told me that he would be unable to travel against it but as it would be at our backs I decided to start. For breakfast I went around to the aranga occupied by the other Russian and made a first rate meal of frozen bear meat, flapjacks and cocoa, topping off with three pipefuls of American tobacco. About ten o'clock we started on our way. We had not gone far before the weather cleared and the wind died down, so that we had a beautiful, clear, cold day and made good progress along the tundra. At sunset we built our igloo, had our pemmican and some deer meat that Kataktovick had procured at Cape North and turned in. Long since we had used up our supply of ship's biscuit, most of which had got damaged beyond use by salt water on the way across the ice from Wrangell Island.

At daylight on April 10 we left our igloo and by the time we got away the sun had risen. It was a fine, clear day, with a light easterly wind, which was very cold. Kataktovick complained of his hands and feet and I suffered a good deal of pain in my arms. The dogs were working badly and were able to travel only with the greatest difficulty,

CHAPTER XXIV

COLT

Shortly after we started, one of the dogs, called Whitey, lay down and refused to work. Poor old Whitey! He had given all there was in him and had worn himself out on the hard travelling from Shipwreck Camp to Wrangell Island and again across Long Strait to Siberia. I unharnessed him, finally, and put him on the sledge. We now had only three dogs left to pull the sledge and our progress was not very fast.

About two o'clock in the afternoon we came upon two more arangas. The native who lived in one of them proved to be a deer man who had hurt himself some time before and was just beginning to feel better. He had seven good dogs which excited my interest. I made signs to show him that we had had seven dogs but had lost all but four, of which one was already too weak to walk, that we were travelling all the way down to East Cape, which I indicated on the chart, and that I wanted some dogs. He was an intelligent man and understood what I was after. He and his household brought out tea, which was very refreshing and invigorating, together with frozen deer meat and walrus meat; Kataktovick ate the walrus meat and I the deer meat. Our host made clear to me that we could not reach another aranga before nightfall and invited us to stop with him. We accepted gladly.

The deer man was loath to part with any of his dogs. Finally he said he would not decide that night but would let me know in the morning. We were up with the first crack of dawn and had a breakfast of pemmican, frozen deer meat and tea; then I reopened the subject of the dogs. The Eskimo said that he would not sell me a dog but would let me take one if I would send it back from East Cape. I gave him a razor and promised to do so. Then he showed me his rifle, which was a Remington, and some cartridges, making signs to ask me if I had any cartridges to pay him for the use of the dog. I had no Remington cartridges, but took out the chart and showed him that after reaching East Cape I was going across to Nome and would send him some cartridges from there. He knew about Nome; evidently the trading motor-boats from Nome had been up along the Siberian coast. The dog, as I understood, I could send back from East Cape by travellers bound west, though the distance was at least three hun-

dred miles as the crow flies. He told me that there
was a white man at Koliuchin Bay and that Mr.
Caraieff, who was a brother of the one I had met
at Cape North, had a fur-trading station at East
Cape.

The deer man was an honorable man as well as
a trustful one. With the exception of a razor and
a pickaxe which I gave him before we left, he received nothing but a promise made him in sign
language, yet he let us have one of his best dogs.
I asked the native who lived in the other aranga if
he would not go with us as far as Koliuchin Bay.
He replied that he could not leave his family for
so long a journey, because they would probably get
nothing to eat. I was sorry for this, but I had been
so warmly welcomed here that I wanted to show
my appreciation, so I gave him a tin of oil to use
with the Primus stove that he had, for which he
had had no oil for a long time.

I tried to write down the name of the native to
whom I owed the cartridges but it defied spelling;
even the experts in phonetic spelling would, I
think, have had trouble with it. Later on, however, when I reached Koliuchin Bay I told Mr.
Olsen, the American trader whom I found there,
about the arrangement I had made and he easily
identified the man. I am glad to say that I have

every reason to believe that the cartridges which I sent him when I finally reached Alaska arrived safely.

With our new dog now harnessed to the sledge and Whitey still a passenger, we got away by the middle of the forenoon and by mid-afternoon reached another aranga, where we found two women. I tried to make them understand that I wanted to see the man of the house and buy a dog from him; there were several pretty good dogs running around outside the aranga. The women were not very talkative but they finally managed to make me understand that the men were away, gathering driftwood. We made ourselves some tea and waited. Kataktovick went into the aranga and presently returned to tell me that the women had some flour and were willing to give us some. I hardly knew what we could do with it and said so.

Kataktovick replied, "Me make flapjacks."

He got some of the flour and mixed it with melted snow. Then he greased the cover of the tea boiler with walrus blubber, placed it over the Primus stove and cooked half a dozen flapjacks. They proved to be very good, and from that time on, whenever we got a chance, we had flapjacks; unfortunately chances like this were few and far between. The day was fine and clear and we had a good view of the hinterland, which, I found, resembled the coast of Grant Land, where I had been on my voyages with Peary in the *Roosevelt*.

Presently the men returned, an old man and his son. I asked him for a dog. He replied—we both, of course, talked in the Esperanto of signs— that he had only seven and did not care to part with any. I had a pair of binoculars which I offered him but could not tempt him, though he was very polite in his refusal to trade. I had with me a new forty-five calibre Colt revolver, with eighty-three cartridges left, which I had used to shoot seal. The boy was standing around while we were carrying on our conversation. I handed him the loaded revolver and made signs to him to try a shot with it. About thirty yards away was a stick, standing up in the snow. The boy fired at it and cut it in two the first shot. He showed his pride and satisfaction plainly and required little urging to try a shot at another stick a little farther away. This time he missed; with the next shot, however, he cut this stick in two. It was good shooting, especially as I do not think he had ever seen a revolver before.

Turning to the boy, I took a dog with one hand and the revolver with the other and made signs that if I could have the dog, the revolver was his. The old man demurred, but the boy took him off where they could talk the matter over and pres-

ently the old man came back and signified that he
would agree to the bargain. Kataktovick looked
over the dog he offered us and we agreed that it
was not much good, so I pointed to a better dog
and indicated that he was my choice. The old man
shook his head but offered to let me have the dog
if I would add the binoculars to the revolver. I
in turn shook my head, took the revolver and the
cartridges from the boy and prepared to leave.
At that the old man gave in and handed over the
dog and a harness; so I gave the revolver and the
cartridges back to the boy, hitched up the dog and
we were soon on our way again. The dog was a
strong, little, white fellow, and worked well. Our
old Whitey was well enough now to trot along behind the sledge, but could do no work yet. Including Whitey we now had six dogs.

It was about three o'clock when we left the old
man's aranga. About sunset, which now came at
seven o'clock, we met a party of Chukches, with
three teams of dogs, bound westward towards Cape
North. We stopped for a few minutes' conversation and I found that they had come from Cape
Onman at the mouth of Koliuchin Bay. They
told me that they would reach the aranga which
we had last left by the time it was dark, which
would be in about an hour and a half. It had
taken us four hours to cover the distance but we

were walking whereas the Siberians had from sixteen to twenty-two dogs to each team and could therefore ride on the sledges and travel at good speed.

Shortly after we passed these men, we stopped and built our igloo for the night. We debated how we should manage about the two new dogs that we had acquired that day, whether we should tether them outside or take them into the igloo with us. I did not feel like taking any chances on leaving them outside so we brought them in, with their harness still on. When we lay down to sleep we tied their traces together and lay on the traces.

We had had a long and active day and soon fell fast asleep. The temperature outside was about fifty below zero. Sometime during the night I woke up, feeling pretty cold. There was a big hole in the side of the igloo. The dogs had worked their way out of the harness and got away. We had some tea and as soon as it became light enough I sent Kataktovick back to the aranga where we had obtained the last dog, which we called Colt; I thought it likely that the other dog would stop there, too. I told Kataktovick to get the man to harness up his sledge and ride back with him to save time. Several hours later Kataktovick came back with Colt and his late owner and we put Colt into our team again. The other dog, however, they

had not seen; evidently he had gone right on. I
gave the man a tin of pemmican for his trouble and
we went on our way again.

It was long after sunset when we built our igloo
for the night. I determined that Colt should not
get away again, so we tied his mouth to prevent
him from chewing his harness and took him into
the igloo with us. In some way, however, he
chewed himself free, broke out of the igloo and
escaped. The distance was now too great to send
back for him and I gave up all hope of ever seeing
him again.

With our dogs again reduced to four, two of
which were of little use, we got away at five o'clock
the next morning. Early in the afternoon we
came upon an old man and a boy, collecting big
logs of driftwood. I asked the old man what he
was going to do with the logs, but could not understand his reply. Perhaps he planned to build a
house or a boat. He had a tent in which he was
living and I gathered he was going to move eastward that afternoon. We made a fire of driftwood and had some tea and then went on. Kataktovick told me that he understood from the old man
that he would probably overtake us later on and
give us a lift with his sledge. Sure enough, a
couple of hours before sunset, he came up with us
and invited us to ride. The snow was light and

powdery and I had been wearing my snowshoes all day. The dogs, too, had made hard going of it on account of the condition of the snow. I accepted the old man's invitation, therefore, to ride on the sledge but after about ten minutes found it so cold sitting still that I got off, resumed my snowshoes and walked.

When it was nearly dark we stopped and set up the old man's big tent. The northwest wind was growing stronger and the snow was drifting. I got the Primus stove going and made tea for all four of us and we all had pemmican. The old man and his son had nothing much of their own to eat.

We were just finishing our supper when the men with the three dog-teams, whom we had passed three days before, came up; they had been to Cape North and were now returning. We filled the Primus stove again, made them some tea and gave them some pemmican to eat. After a while they informed me that they had the white dog Colt that had got away from us. The old man had sent him back by them. I was taken completely by surprise and to say that I was glad to see him would be putting it mildly. Nothing could have exceeded that old man's honesty and generosity; once he had gone to the trouble of bringing Colt back himself, and now he had sent him back. It was simply one of the many instances of fine humanity which I met with among these Chukches. All honor and gratitude to them!

The new arrivals and ourselves sat in the tent and attempted conversation. They were sociable and friendly, like all the others whom we met, but Kataktovick, as I afterwards learned, never quite succeeded in conquering his misgivings. It was difficult to make them understand and sometimes I would get excited and talk in loud and emphatic tones. This would arouse Kataktovick's fears and he would say: "You must not talk that way." He was afraid they would misunderstand my earnestness and take offense. The same thing had happened before and Kataktovick was always afraid of the consequences.

On the fourteenth we had a high westerly gale. The men with the three dog teams got away before we did. They said our dogs were slow and they were in a hurry. I tried to buy a dog from them with my binoculars but could not tempt them.

Leaving the old man and his son in their big tent we left early in the morning, with the high wind at our backs, and made fairly good going all day. At noon we reached an aranga and had some tea. Then we went on again and about five o'clock came to another aranga. Near by was an empty tent. We entered and in a few minutes an old man came in from the aranga and made signs that he

would make us some tea if we wanted it. He went
back to the aranga and presently returned with a
brand new copper kettle, holding about two gallons. He said we could use it and that he would
get the ice to fill it if we would provide the fire and
the tea. I saw that it was going to take some time
to make tea, so we went along, but as the old man
seemed to be pretty badly off I gave him some
pemmican and tea tablets.

At dark we built our igloo. I took Colt inside with us and tied his mouth, taking a half
hitch on the rope so that he could not chew. Then
I put three or four turns of the rope criss-cross on
the harness so that he could not extricate himself,
and tied the rope to myself. The result was that
with his continuous restlessness I got no sleep all
night. It was the last time I tried that device;
after that I simply tethered him with the rest of
the dogs.

CHAPTER XXV

"MUSIC HATH CHARMS"

The next morning dawned clear and fine. We got away early and had good going, so that by noon we reached an aranga not far from Cape Wankarem. We were received kindly here and given tea, which was all that the house afforded. I left some tea tablets in exchange.

Proceeding on our way again we reached Cape Wankarem at five o'clock in the afternoon; the cape is not high land, just a low promontory. We found four arangas here. Our usual method when we came to a place with more than one aranga was to look the whole collection over and go to what seemed the most likely one of the lot. Here, therefore, we passed one or two which seemed only ordinary and stopped before the one which seemed the best. An old man came out and made signs for us to enter. We did so and as soon as we were inside the door an old woman took us in charge. She removed our boots and stockings, turned them inside out and hung them up to dry over the native lamp. Then she brought out her best china and we had tea with sugar in it. She had two fine-looking daughters who helped wait upon us. The aranga was scrupulously clean, with plenty of furs; evidently the master of the house was in comfortable circumstances.

When we had finished our tea the old man made signs that he wanted to see my chart; clearly the men who had gone on ahead of us, the previous day, had told him about us, and he wanted to see for himself. I brought out the chart and showed it to him. He examined it carefully and made signs about the crushing of the ship. Presently he went to a box and produced a number of magazines, perhaps ten or a dozen in all, most of them about two years old. There were copies of *The World's Work, The National Geographic Magazine, The Literary Digest* and *The Illustrated London News*. The day's march in the cold wind, following the long succession of such days, with the hours of searching through the whirling snowdrift for the right path from Wrangell Island and the glare of the sun along the tundra, had affected my eyes more and more severely. By this time, besides being pretty tired and sleepy, I felt more like giving my eyes a rest than trying to read. I could hardly make out the print and it hurt my eyes a good deal, so I made signs to our host and he understood at once and did not urge the magazines upon me.

Fortunately, too, relief came in the person of another old man, who entered the aranga just then. He was evidently a crony of our host, for without more ado both fell to playing casino, like a couple of old veterans playing cards in their club.

After a time, I fell asleep and had a refreshing nap. When I awoke, the card-players were still at it. After a while they finished their game and then our host got out a box. It looked very much like a talking-machine and I remember thinking, "What in the name of Heaven is that?" Then he removed a cloth from another box and took out a record and I saw that it was indeed a talking-machine. The old man acted just like an American householder who proudly plays you the latest record by Caruso or John McCormack. He treated us to an extended concert, numbering forty-two selections, starting off with "My Hero" from "The Chocolate Soldier." About half of the songs were in Russian and the rest in English. Like the true music-lover, he kept on playing until he had finished all of his forty-two records, while the old lady busied herself mending our clothes. I was so sleepy that I am afraid I dropped off several times during the concert but I enjoyed it just the same.

The old man now passed over to me a tumbler and a spoon, together with a bottle which contained some kind of patent "painkiller." Then he brought out a sick boy about fifteen years old and made signs to me to give the youngster a dose of the painkiller. The tumbler and spoon and bottle were all carefully wrapped up in a neat package and I could see that the old man prized this medicine kit of his as much as an Arctic explorer might value a medal. The directions on the bottle were printed in English. As nearly as I could find out, the boy had received his last treatment some time during the previous summer; evidently the doses were given him only when some one happened along who could read the directions. I took the bottle and the spoon and measured out the proper quantity in the glass, added water and administered it to my patient in a very solemn manner, just as if I were a real doctor. I don't suppose there was enough of it to do the youngster any real harm; certainly he did not receive medical attention often enough to do him permanent injury. I was very deliberate in my actions; in fact I believe I consumed fully half an hour in the process.

I enjoyed here the best night's sleep I had had since I had left Shipwreck Camp, nearly two months before. In the morning the old woman presented me with a fine pair of deerskin mittens. I gave her a gill-net. To the boy I gave a pocket compass and divided a yard or two of ribbon between the girls. We got away shortly after daylight. Our treatment at the kind hands of this Chukch family will always remain in my memory.

The old man seemed to realize that we had great need for getting along as fast as we could and he volunteered to give us a lift to the next aranga nine or ten miles away. He said nothing about going until he harnessed up his dogs just as we were starting. It was a great help and enabled us to get along so well that we covered the distance by nine o'clock. At this next aranga we met four Russian prospectors who were on their way from East Cape to Cape North, near which are gold mines. They were well-equipped travellers. Each had a sledge with a team of twelve fine dogs. They treated us to black bread, butter, tea, sugar and sardines. One of them could speak a little English; he wrote his name for me on a piece of paper which, I am sorry to say, I lost.

We had two snow-knives with us and when we now said goodby to the old native who had been so kind to us, I gave him one of these, with a couple of steel drills which we used for making holes for the sledge-shoes, and a skein of fish-line.

Travelling all day long, we came some time after the sun went down to a place where there were three arangas. The Russian miners had told us about them and had said they thought we should be able to reach them by nightfall. Two of the arangas were close together and the third was off by itself. The people here were less hospitably inclined than those whom we had met before and, though they did not actually tell us to keep away, they did not volunteer any invitation to enter. It was dark and we had come a long distance, so I did not feel like spending an hour building an igloo for shelter for the night; I went up to one of the arangas, therefore, and when a young man came out I made signs that we should like to stop there. When we finally got inside I understood why the people were not especially glad to see us. They had evidently had hard luck and had very little food, even for themselves. While Kataktovick was outside feeding the dogs, I got the Primus stove going, made some tea and passed it around, with pemmican.

There was a young woman here, with a baby two or three months old who was evidently sick; he was what would be described, I believe, as "fussy." His mother would get him quiet and then he would cry out and to my great surprise she would get very angry and shake him violently; then she would repent and would croon to him, only to repeat the shaking when the poor little fellow cried out again. In all my long experience with Eskimo I had never before seen a woman even speak a cross word to her child.

Perhaps she could not get along with her mother-in-law and took it out on her baby. At all events the mother-in-law, who was very old, was a tough customer. Quite unknowingly I sat down in her place and fell asleep. Some time after midnight I was awakened by a smart slap on the cheek. I was too drowsy to pay much attention to this but presently was brought up broad awake by having the old woman step on my face. I found her snorting and grunting; the young mother was still crooning and talking to the baby. I had all my clothes on, so I shook Kataktovick and we went outdoors.

The light was just showing along the eastern horizon. We made a little snow shelter, had some tea and pemmican and started on our way about two o'clock in the morning. We travelled hard all day. There was a strong northwest gale and the air was filled with drifting snow so that we could not see very far ahead. When we came to Cape Onman we were disappointed to find no arangas there; only the framework was left and we found out later that the people had moved to Koliuchin Island. We kept along the trail, which to our surprise took us away from the land and out on to the ice on the broad entrance to Koliuchin Bay, and presently we came to Koliuchin Island, a high formation, like a warship bottom up.

Here we found ten or a dozen arangas and visible signs of prosperity. A young man came out on our approach and said, "Me speek 'em plenty English. Me know Nome. Me know trader well. Me spend long time East Cape. You come in aranga. Me speak 'em plenty. You get plenty eat here."

We went in. It was a well-appointed Siberian home, occupied jointly by two young men and their families. The men were deer men, with fine herds of reindeer twelve or fourteen days' journey into the interior. We had some tea and some frozen deer meat. Then the women cooked us some seal meat, which was excellent. The older man's wife made flapjacks out of flour and they tasted good.

These people had evidently heard about us and they knew our desire to get to East Cape, for after we had finished eating, the native who had first greeted us said, "I bring you East Cape; how much?"

I asked him how many dogs he had. He told me, and said he had a good sledge, too, and could get us to East Cape in five days, if we were to start at once.

I had with me forty-five dollars which Mr. Hadley had lent me when I left Wrangell Island. Naturally I wanted to keep this sum intact as long as possible. To get to East Cape in five days, however, would justify me in parting with my money.

"How much you pay me?" the man asked again.

"Forty dollars," I replied, for the trip seemed to me well worth that. It was a mistake; I should have said twenty. Forty was so large a sum that the native soon made clear that he doubted my having so much money. He was a trader, for reindeer skins and fox skins, and he knew, or thought he knew, how a bargain should be made.

"All right," he said. "You show me money."

"No," I replied.

"Maybe you no have money," he ventured.

"I have the money," I answered.

In his anxiety to see that I should not suffer in the Chukch's estimation, Kataktovick now started to explain to him about the money and I had to stop him.

"You bring me East Cape me give you forty dollars."

The Chukch seemed satisfied. It was agreed that we should leave our sledge and about all our possessions and that we should journey onward on the deer man's sledge. At Koliuchin Bay we should find an American trader, Mr. Olsen, about whom I had been hearing all along the coast. As far as Mr. Olsen's the other deer man was to accompany us with his sledge, Kataktovick riding with him; for this service he was to receive a hatchet, a piece of tent canvas and two tins of pemmican.

The next morning, April 19, Kataktovick complained of pains in his legs and wanted to stay where we were for a day to rest. I did not object to the idea and was glad of an opportunity of resting the dogs.

That night our prospective tourist conductor began talking again about the money. Evidently he was worried, or else his conscience pricked him.

"By and by you meet Olsen," he said. "He white man. Perhaps he tell you you pay me too much money. You no pay me."

I replied that whatever Mr. Olsen might tell me would make no difference, that I had promised to pay and I would. I refused to let him see the money, however, though he was itching to get a look at it. "You no trust me, I no trust you," I said.

Then he voiced the age-old cry of the savage against the civilized; the pity of it is that the savage is right.

"White man steal from other man," he said. "White man promise bring things for fox skins and bear skins. White man no bring 'em. White man go 'way, forget come back."

CHAPTER XXVI

WE ARRIVE AT EAST CAPE

The next morning, April 19, we started off with
the two sledges. I had our own dogs harnessed in
the team that drew the sledge on which I rode and
had with me the pemmican that we had left and
other essentials, so that about all that we finally
left behind was our sledge. I should have liked to
keep the sledge and bring it all the way home with
me, but the Chukches liked the looks of it and they
would find it useful in travelling over the rough ice.
I could get along without it, and I was beginning
now to feel the long strain and wanted to hurry on
by the fastest means possible.

As we travelled, two to each sledge, one man
would ride while the other walked. The sledges
used by the natives, from Cape North east, are
about sixteen feet long, two-and-a-half feet wide
and eight inches high. The framework is light
and rather crudely made. The runners are four
inches wide. When the snow is hard they do not
use steel shoes; instead they coat the runners with
ice. They always keep a bottle of water inside
their clothing and carry a piece of bearskin with

them. At frequent intervals during the day they pour water on the bearskin and rub it over the runners; it freezes quickly and forms a coating of ice which reduces the friction, whereas a steel shoe in extreme cold has a tendency to cling to the snow. When the weather gets warm enough so that the snow is at the melting stage they use the steel shoes.

They seldom use a whip; instead they are more likely to use a stick about three feet long with a heavy spear-point on the end. Along this stick are several rings which jingle and rattle against each other and make the dogs quicken their speed. They use this stick as a brake when the sledge is going down hill, setting it up at the forward end and letting the spear-point scratch along; in this way they keep the sledge from running over the dogs. They have large teams of dogs and can get over the ground rapidly. If all went well we should now be able to make far greater progress than had been possible with our small number of worn-out dogs.

We went back across the entrance to Koliuchin Bay to Cape Onman and followed the bay shore to a point about fifteen miles from Mr. Olsen's place. About two hours before we reached the aranga where we were to spend the night my guide stopped the sledge and informed me that he was not going to East Cape with me. He said he would go on to the aranga and the other man would take us on to Mr. Olsen's place and then we could go on by ourselves.

"How about the forty dollars?" I asked. "Don't you want it?"

He had been thinking things over, he said, and he had decided that as he had a lot of deerskins back in the country and must get them before some one else did, the money I had agreed to pay him was not enough to compensate him for the risk he would take, for if he went clear through to East Cape he would get back too late. The fact was, as I could easily see, that he knew that forty dollars was much too high a price for the job he had undertaken, and he was afraid that if I got to a place where I could talk with some white man about it, I would learn that and refuse to pay. Apparently he had little confidence in a white man's word.

I listened to the explanation he offered about the deerskins and said, "All right,—we will let it go at that."

We came to our stopping-place on the western shore of Koliuchin Bay late in the afternoon. The man who lived in the aranga came out and asked me in. I saw to it that everything that I had on the sledge was taken off and put in the aranga and that our five dogs were fed and cared for. I was just pulling off my boots and stockings when the man from Koliuchin Island came in and said, "Me want money to bring you here."

"Not a cent!" I answered. He was silent for some time. Then I decided that I would show him that I could be a good sport, so I said I would give him five dollars. I showed him the forty-five dollars that I carried with me and said that if he had taken me to East Cape he would have had the four ten-dollar bills. He said never a word but took the five-dollar bill that I handed over to him and without waiting to thank me started back over the road. And now we had no sledge.

That night I made a bargain with another native to get us to Mr. Olsen's place, giving him as pay a snow-knife, a small pickaxe and two steel drills. We left at early dawn the next morning, travelling with all our goods and chattels on the sledge. Our dogs were harnessed with his, though they were so tired that they could barely keep up.

About noon we reached Mr. Olsen's place. Mr. Olsen, I found, was a naturalized American citizen, thirty-eight years old, a trader known all up and down the coast. He was the agent of Mr. Olaf Swenson of Seattle, who was later to play so important a part in the rescue of our men.

The summer before he had learned of our expedition from Mr. Swenson and others who had been up to Koliuchin Bay with supplies. It was

a great surprise to him to see me here now. His
hospitality was unbounded; everything he had was
at our disposal. He made some tea for us at once,
and offered us bread, also made by himself, which
was as good as any I have ever eaten. I am
ashamed to think of the amount of this bread that
I ate; no Christmas cake or plum pudding ever
tasted better. After our meal I enjoyed a smoke
of his good tobacco and then we turned in. Mr.
Olsen made me take his own bunk and I had a refreshing sleep.

The man who had accompanied us here now
went back, so the next morning, after a good deal
of trouble, Mr. Olsen got another man with a sledge
and a dog team. With the exception of Colt, our
dogs were still very tired. Most of the dogs be-
longing to the people at Koliuchin Bay were away
in various directions hunting. Mr. Olsen used his
influence, however, and we were able to get away in
good season, with a good sledge and a full dog-
team. The driver and ourselves all took turns;
two of us would walk while the other rode.

During the day we passed Pitlekaj, the point
where the *Vega,* Nordenskiöld's ship, on the voyage
on which she made the Northeast Passage, became
frozen in the ice, on September 28, 1878, when only
a few days' run from Bering Strait and scarcely
six miles from open water, and did not again get

free until July 18, 1879.   The *Vega,* fortunately, encountered no such terrific gale as that which drove the *Karluk* westward in September, 1913, but her mishap in being frozen in the ice was quite as unexpected and her situation quite as uncontrollable.

Several times during the day's march we stopped at an aranga for tea.   At six o'clock we reached an aranga near Idlidlija Island.   We were now half way from Koliuchin Bay to Cape Serdze. For his services I paid the old man who had accompanied us here a small spade, two packages of tobacco and an order on Mr. Olsen for fifteen dollars' worth of supplies.   I had now given away nearly all the things we had had with us when we started from Wrangell Island.

After another restful night and a good meal of salmon, we left early the next morning, April 22, for Cape Serdze.   By a little bargaining I had obtained the services of a native with his sledge and dogs and as I found another native about to start on his way eastward at the same time I got him to take Kataktovick along with him.   This arrangement gave us two men to each sledge, which would result in better progress.

It was a wonderful day.   The temperature was only a little below the freezing-point and the sun's rays were distinctly warm.   The sunlight, in fact, coupled with the glare of the snow, was hard on my eyes. At Koliuchin Island I had had an Eskimo woman make me a cap out of Burberry cloth that we had with us, with a three-inch vizor of sealskin, supported by copper wire around the rim. I wore my hood over this cap and could adjust the vizor at any angle; this afforded some relief to my eyes.

At three o'clock in the afternoon we arrived at Cape Serdze. Here we were met by Mr. Wall, a Norwegian, of about forty, who was an electrical engineer, by profession, had lived in the United States and knew people in Boston and New York whom I knew. He lived in a very comfortable aranga but there was sickness in the house so, with apologies for his inability to entertain us, he sent us to an aranga owned by a native who went by the name of Corrigan, the best-known hunter in Siberia. Corrigan showed me some of the results of his season's hunting, which included fifteen or twenty fine polar-bear skins and a large number of skins of the white fox. He was by far the most prosperous native I had met. Mr. Wall sent me over some bread and tea and milk, with some excellent griddle-cakes.

With Mr. Wall's assistance I was able to obtain the services of Corrigan to take us to East Cape, a distance of about ninety miles. I left here everything that would be of no further use to us, for I knew now that during the remainder of our journey we should be able to get anything we needed. With the exception of the day when we got to Koliuchin Island we had had fine weather all the way from Cape North; now it was even better because every day the sun was getting higher and its heat more perceptible.

From Cape Serdze eastward the water is deep near the shore and the travelling in places along the sea-ice was rough, because the drift ice came close to shore. We had a good many steep inclines to go down and had exciting experiences, especially as we went along at top speed. Corrigan, however, was a daring and capable dog-driver, and knew how to steer the sledge as well as a man can steer a ship. He had sixteen dogs, all of the very best quality, and where the going was good we travelled very fast. Corrigan had a chum who went along with us with some of Corrigan's dogs and ours. Kataktovick travelled with this other man.

At several points along the way we passed groups of arangas perched on shelves projecting out from the face of the cliffs, a hundred feet above the shore. In some cases it was hard to see how the natives could climb up into them; they reminded me of pictures I had seen of the homes of the cliff-dwellers. The natives live on these heights because they want to be on the coast near the walrus and seal and can find no other location for their arangas.

We made fifty miles during the day. It was light nearly all of the twenty-four hours now and we were able to keep going until seven o'clock in the evening, before stopping at a very comfortable aranga for the night.

Sitting on the sledge so long, when I had not been used to it, made my back ache and the pain was so great that I did not sleep at all; in fact, I had a miserable night. The air in the aranga, too, was very hot.

The next day we got away shortly after daybreak. The going was rough in many places and we had to travel close under the cliffs. It was a warm day, with a temperature about freezing; where the sun's rays struck the angles of the cliffs water was dropping. There was, in fact, a good deal of danger in passing along under the cliffs, for the heat of the sun was releasing the boulders that the frost had dislodged during the winter and now they came tearing down the face of the cliff without warning straight across our path.

As we journeyed on the pleasant warmth of the sun's rays made the ride a rather more enjoyable excursion than we had been experiencing before on our travels. At times Corrigan and I attempted conversation. He could speak very little English

and though I had picked up a few phrases along
the coast I could speak no native language that he
could understand. He was considered the dare-
devil of northern Siberia and had such a reputation
for taking chances that it was said that when Corrigan could not get a bear it was because bear were
scarce and it would not be worth while for any one
else to try. Mr. Wall had told Corrigan what I
had said about our voyage and shipwreck and our
experiences since. Now, while we were riding
along, Corrigan would start in to tell me of his
exploits. I knew just enough of the language to
recognize an occasional word when he described
hunting the walrus and polar bear and the narrow es-
capes he had had on the drift ice and hunting whale
in skin-boats with the harpoon. He would get
more and more excited, and finally I would cease to
understand anything and could do nothing but nod at
frequent intervals, until he would become aware
of my total ignorance of what he was saying; then
he would put his hands to his head, with a gesture
of despair. He became greatly excited and irri-
tated when he found that neither of us could relate
his adventures to the other. It was all very amus-
ing to me, especially as when I had first heard his
name mentioned I had thought of him as an Irish-
man.

Stopping at intervals along the way to have tea

in the various arangas that we passed, we finally reached Emma Town, a few miles to the southwest of East Cape, at about six P. M. The second stage of our journey from Wrangell Island was over. We had been thirty-seven days on the march and probably had actually travelled about seven hundred miles, all but the last part of the way on foot. There now remained the question of transportation to Alaska, and the sooner I was able to arrange for that the better.

CHAPTER XXVII

At Emma Town I found the brother of the Mr. Caraieff whom I had met at Cape North. I presented my letter of introduction and was hospitably received. Mr. Caraieff, I found, was a graduate of a college at Vladivostock. He was able to carry on a conversation with me in quite intelligible English and had no difficulty in understanding me. He invited me to stay at his home as long as I liked. I thanked him but said that I must get over to the American shore as soon as possible.

We talked over ways and means. The ice in Bering Strait, I found, had broken up so that I should be unable to get across by sledge; later on I could get a whaleboat, he said, with some Eskimo, to take me across to the Diomede Islands and from there another whale-boat or a skin-boat to get across to Cape Prince of Wales. That would be some time in May, just when would depend entirely on the amount of ice in the waters of the Strait. The present was a kind of between-season time when it was too late for sledges and too early for boats. It would be June before any ships would get to East Cape.

It seemed to me that my best chance of getting immediately in touch with Ottawa would be to go south to Anadyr and send a message from the wireless station there. Mr. Caraieff was inclined to think that the season was already so advanced that I would not really save any time in that way, because the ice would be breaking up in the rivers that I must cross on the way and there was an even chance that when I reached Anadyr I might find that the wireless was out of commission, in which event my journey would be in vain. At Emma Harbor on Providence Bay was a Mr. Thompson, he said, who had a schooner with a gasoline engine. He would be leaving for Nome the first week in June and would take me with him.

Thinking things over I felt that the trip to Anadyr would be worth the risk, for even if the wireless were out of commission there I could still get across to Nome, so the next day, with Mr. Caraieff's assistance, I made all arrangements with some natives to take me to Indian Point, where I could get some other natives to take me on to Anadyr. We planned to start in a day or so and I considered the matter settled, when over night, so to speak, came a rapidly increasing swelling in my legs and feet, due, I suppose, to the punishment they had received, and before I realized it I found myself a helpless invalid, forced to accept Mr. Caraieff's kind hospitality.

My host had a Russian servant by the name of Koshimuroff, who was most assiduous in his efforts to restore my legs to their normal condition, massaging them faithfully at Mr. Caraieff's direction. He filled a large pork-barrel about half full of warm water and I took the first bath I had had since I left Shipwreck Camp. He also cut my hair, what there was left of it; the constant use of the hood had literally worn much of it off the top of my head; several months elapsed before it grew out again. I also shaved, and when I saw myself in the looking-glass, after shaving and having my hair cut, I hardly recognized myself.

My stay here was made pleasant by the opportunity I had, when my eyes became more nearly normal, to read the magazines which Mr. Charles Carpendale, an Australian-born trader, with a station at the same place as Mr. Caraieff's, brought me. These had been sent across from Nome the previous summer and were not what might be described in the language of the train-boy as "all the latest magazines," but they were a pleasure to me, just the same, as they are to all the traders who are scattered up and down the Siberian coast.

The third day after my arrival I was sitting

alone in the front room of Mr. Caraieff's house when in walked a Russian gentleman who shook hands with me and introduced himself in English as Baron Kleist, the Supervisor of Northeastern Siberia. He passed on in search of my host and shortly afterwards returned with him and we all sat and talked, while I showed the Baron my charts. I had been looking for him for several days, for I knew that he had left his home at Emma Harbor shortly after New Year's Day and had been on an inspection trip, across country to Koliuchin Bay and eastward along the coast, ever since. He was now bound home again.

He had heard of me from Mr. Olsen at Koliuchin Bay and had been told by him that I was a man of fifty-five or so. "I see that you are much younger than I was told you were," he said. Later on in the progress of our pleasant acquaintance, as I began to show the good effects of rest and substantial food, he said, "You're getting younger every day. After all there is not much difference in our ages." He was a man of about forty, only a few years older than myself.

He told us all the news. It was two months old but I had heard hardly any news of the outside world for nearly a year. Nothing unusual had happened or seemed likely to happen. Peace reigned everywhere. He told us of the discovery

the previous year of Nicholas II Land off the Taimir Peninsula by the Russian ships *Taimir* and
Vaigatch under the command of Captain Vilkitski,
an achievement of which as a Russian he might be
justly proud.

Baron Kleist discussed with me the best course
for me to pursue in getting word to the Canadian
Government. He planned to leave about May 10
for Emma Harbor, he said, and he asked me to go
along with him and be his guest at his home. Mr.
Caraieff from Cape North had come to East Cape
about the time the baron arrived, and I had made
arrangements for him to take me to Emma Harbor,
so it was arranged that we should all travel together.
Kataktovick I would leave at East Cape; we had
taken him on at Point Barrow, but he said he
wanted to go to Point Hope. I could give him
provisions and outfit enough to last him for some
time and, after navigation opened, he could get a
ship to take him across to Point Hope.

Corrigan went back to Cape Serdze. Before
he left he begged very hard for my binoculars, so
I finally gave them to him on condition that he
would never part with them; this he promised
faithfully.

My rest was gradually putting me in condition
to travel again. At first I was almost as helpless
as a child. I suffered no pain, but the swelling in

my legs and feet was severe and I seemed to have lost every bit of energy I had ever possessed. My eyes were bloodshot and I was so' stiff I could hardly move hand or foot. Kataktovick had little swelling but suffered a good deal of pain in his legs. We were both pretty thin; I had lost thirty or forty pounds and Kataktovick was equally worn down.

Before I began to recover from this swelling of the legs, I developed an acute attack of tonsilitis. It was the first trouble of the kind that I had experienced in all my Arctic work. I recall that on the North Pole expedition, while we were encamped at Cape Sheridan and most of us were away on hunting trips, MacMillan and Doctor Goodsell opened a case of books and both came down with violent head colds. The books were brand new books, too; apparently they had been packed by a man with a cold. The baron had a clinical thermometer with him and he found that my temperature was well above normal. My throat was ulcerated and sore but I used peroxide and alum and after a time the infection subsided.

When the tenth of May came, however, the tonsilitis was still with me and I was conscious that it had weakened my whole system for the time being, in addition to the physical weariness of which the swelling in my legs and feet was a symptom.

The baron was anxious to get away, for the season was advancing, and, at any moment, a thaw might set in which would· break up the ice in the rivers and interfere with the journey. My legs and feet had more strength in them by now but I could not walk as well as usual. So it was decided that, as we were now ready, we might as well start.

Kataktovick saw us off; we were parting, here. I thanked him, as I bade him good-by, for all that he had done, and told him how greatly I was indebted to him for his constant help and for his faith and trust in me. The money due him would be paid to him later on, I said, after I had got back to civilization. I asked Mr. Carpendale to tell the Chukches what a good boy Kataktovick was. I gave him the rifle we had carried on our journey and some other things we had with us, and then we shook hands warmly and parted.

The day was not a cold one; the thermometer, in fact, was about freezing and there was a good deal of fog. Consequently, the travelling was not so easy as it might have been but we had good dogs and good drivers, and, as we had postponed our start until the late afternoon when the snow was beginning to get harder, we made considerable progress before we stopped at ten P. M. at an aranga for tea and bear meat. We then kept on our way until four o'clock in the morning—the light was sufficient now for travelling all through the twenty-four hours—and then we reached another aranga, where we slept. We had intended to make an aranga still further on before stopping but the snow was soft and the fog was so thick that we had difficulty in telling where we were, so we decided not to risk too much in the face of such adverse weather conditions but to stop while we could.

We drank our tea and turned in. At about eleven A. M. we awoke and breakfasted on some things we had brought with us from East Cape. It was now snowing very hard and there was no use in setting out, so we decided to wait until night. At six P. M. it was snowing harder than ever, so there was nothing to do but to have supper and turn in again. During the day I read a good deal. Mr. Carpendale had given the baron some books and now, as later on in the journey, when I could not sleep I would read. I recall that at this time I was absorbed in Robert Hichens's "Bella Donna." The light inside the aranga was poor so I bundled myself up in my furs and sat in the outer apartment among the dogs and sledges where I could see.

My own dogs I had left with Mr. Caraieff at East Cape. He agreed to keep them until I should want them again. The problem of feeding our dogs along the way to Emma Harbor promised to be a fairly pressing one and so it proved; in fact, the baron was constantly worried by it. The season had advanced and the supply of meat which the natives had laid in during the previous fall was beginning to be exhausted.

The snow turned again to rain during the night of the twelfth and it looked very much as if we should be unable to travel. My throat was gradually getting better but was still sore and painful. We ate a good supper of reindeer meat well cooked by the baron and went to bed.

Not long after midnight the rain held up and the wind, which had shifted to the northwest, cleared the air and lowered the temperature, so that a crust formed on the snow and the going was fairly good. We got away at about two o'clock on the morning of May 13, and for a while made good time, but before long the wind dropped and veered to the southeast, bringing in a pelting rain from Bering Sea. I had tried to get an oilskin coat at East Cape but could find none to fit me; my fur clothing got soaked through after a while and, though it was a rather warm rain, I was afraid of a recurrence of the tonsilitis. Occasionally I dropped off the sledge for exercise to keep warm but my legs were still weak and I could not keep up with the dogs, so I had to get on again and ride. As the tempera-

ture grew colder the rain turned to a very wet snowstorm, accompanied by a thick fog. We could
hardly see ahead of the dogs and steered altogether
by compass.

We were bound for a reindeer settlement half
way along the north side of St. Lawrence Bay
and after a while we brought up at what seemed
to the natives a place they knew; on looking
around, however, they discovered that they were
uncertain where they were. Working our way
along slowly, we finally got out to the slopes of the
bay shore and stopped. The Eskimo were deep
in a discussion of where they were and, as the
baron told me, seemed clear enough about it, when
suddenly the dogs started, pell-mell. I managed
to drop on to the sledge and before I could do
more than catch my breath we were tearing down
hill at a terrific pace. The dogs had scented the
reindeer and had started in their direction without
more ado. How we got along without being flung
bodily against the numerous boulders that lined our
pathway and killed outright, I never knew; we
reached the bottom of the slope without a mishap.
Here we came across a trail which brought us to
the settlement.

The reindeer here were the first I had seen in
Siberia; they had spent the winter inland, but now
that spring was opening they had come out to the

coast. The two young men who owned them were
fine, tall fellows, somewhat resembling North
American Indians; they had been out with their
reindeer in all weathers during the winter, sometimes, the baron told me, for three days in succession, and their faces were burned almost black with
cold and exposure. They were very hospitable
and, as they had just cooked some reindeer meat
as we dropped in, they gave us an enjoyable meal.
My appetite was beginning to come back and my
throat, in spite of the rain and fog, was better.

Refreshed and reassured as to our progress we
started on our way again, crossing the ice of St.
Lawrence Bay and following its shores to the east.
We then went across the land for several miles and
out on to the ice in the mouth of Mechigme Bay.
This journey was full of interest to me. I rode
most of the time and could give myself up to the
enjoyment of the wild country through which we
were passing. The distance from East Cape to
Emma Harbor is about the same as that from New
York to Boston. We averaged four or five miles
an hour. Our dog-drivers were skilful and knew
what they were about; their conversation was unin-
telligible to me but I had every confidence in their
ability.

One of our drivers was about four feet tall; in an
Anglo-Saxon community, I suppose, he would have

been known as Goliath, but among these more literal-minded Siberians he was called "Little." He had a small motor-boat at Indian Point and, if I could not get a ship at Emma Harbor, it would be a great convenience for Little if I went across to Alaska in his motor-boat, because he wanted to go over to Nome, anyway, when the season was far enough advanced for the voyage and I could be navigator, an arrangement which, as a possibility, was quite agreeable to me.

Little, like Artemus Ward's bear, was "an amoosin' little cuss." He could manage to understand pidgin English and was well pleased with himself over it. "Me make baron speak plenty English," he would say.

From Mechigme Bay we followed the coast west for a short distance and then crossed the mouth of the bay to the south shore; following the coast for about twenty miles we went across the land to Neegchan. It was foggy all the time and when we reached a group of arangas at a place called Mesigman and stopped to sleep, I was wet to the skin. The aranga where we were entertained, however, was warm and comfortable; I took off my clothes, wrapped myself in a nice deerskin robe and went to sleep.

At six o'clock in the afternoon we started on again. The weather had cleared up and the surface of the snow was hard, so the going was wonderfully good. For some time we travelled over the sea-ice and had to make a wide detour to avoid a long lane of open water. We stopped once at an aranga on the way for tea and at four o'clock reached a place called Elewn. Here we stayed until six o'clock in the afternoon, when we again got away for an all-night journey.

We were now on the last lap and the dogs knew it, so they travelled at even greater speed than before. At one point as we were going along, we met a Chukch woman driving a team of dogs. Our drivers stopped and talked with her. The baron asked me what I thought about her; his question rather puzzled me but I replied that I supposed the woman was driving the dogs and doing other things that men do, just as I had been accustomed to see women doing among the other Eskimo whom I had known. Then he said that, on the contrary, this was really not a woman at all but a man who had, so to speak, turned himself into a woman. It was, it seemed, a custom among these Siberians to do this and a man who thus transformed himself acted like a woman, dressed like a woman, talked like a woman and was looked upon by the other Chukches as a woman. The baron knew the whys and wherefores of this extraordinary custom but

when he tried to explain it to me his English proved
unequal to the occasion.

Several times during the day we stopped to have
tea. At one place the Eskimo told us that they
had seen or heard of a whaler at Indian Point.
The master was Captain Pederson, they said, but
when they described the ship, their account did not
tally with the description of the *Elvira,* the ship
that Captain Pederson commanded when the *Karluk* left Nome. It was afterwards to be made
known to me that the *Elvira* had been crushed and
sunk off the northern coast of Alaska the previous
fall, during the stormy season when we were being
driven offshore in the *Karluk,* and that Captain
Pederson had made his way overland to Fairbanks,
had thence gone to San Francisco and taken command of another ship, the *Herman.*

After we left the ice of Chechokium we crossed
the divide to Emma Harbor. The mist lay low
over the high mountains on the peninsula between
Emma Harbor and Providence Bay. From time
to time the wind would roll this mist away and
reveal the peaks, stern and forbidding. The going
up the divide was steep and we had a hard climb;
when we got to the top I could look down to
Emma Harbor and see open water out into Providence Bay. The land was white with snow and the

ice nearer shore was unbroken, so that the open water beyond seemed as black as coal-tar, shining against the white. We went down the other side of the ridge at a terrific rate, the dogs running free and the sledge, with the brake-pole grinding hard, careening from side to side in a way that almost took a man's breath away.

It was at seven o'clock on the morning of May 16 that we reached Emma Harbor and the home of Baron Kleist. We had been six days coming from East Cape and two months had gone by since I had parted from the men on Icy Spit, Wrangell Island. If all went well I should be back for them in two months more and I hoped they were holding out all right and would be in good shape when I reached them again. Their suspense, I knew, would be acute until they were sure that I had succeeded in crossing Long Strait to Siberia and getting over to Alaska.

Baron Kleist had a fine house at Emma Harbor. It was well built of heavy timbers, the materials having been brought from Vladivostock five years before. It cost about fifteen thousand dollars, I believe, and was warm and comfortable. The baron had an excellent chef and we enjoyed a substantial breakfast, which in almost no time after our arrival had been prepared for us. Then the baron's own physician, Doctor Golovkoff, who had been with him through the Russo-Japanese War, looked after my legs and throat. He took me under his especial care during my stay and had me in pretty good condition by the time I left.

It was a pleasure for me to find myself once more in a comfortable home. The baroness was spending the winter visiting her relatives in Russia but the numerous touches of a feminine hand were unmistakable throughout the establishment.

At Emma Harbor I met Mr. Thompson, who had a trading-store there. Born on the Baltic, he had been a sea-faring man in his earlier days, serving in German, French and English ships, and could speak English very well. He told me that Captain Pederson had been in the neighborhood with his new ship, the *Herman,* and through him I got a Chukch to take a letter to the captain, telling him where I was and asking him if it would be possible for him to call for me and take me across to the American shore.

Mr. Caraieff had a brother at Indian Point and the latter came over from his trading-station there to see us. He stayed a day or two and when he went home he took a letter for Captain Pederson. I sent out several other letters by Chukches to catch Captain Pederson and, in this way, the news of my desire to get in touch with him spread among the natives along the coast.

CHAPTER XXVIII

On the morning of May 19 an Eskimo whom we had sent over to John Holland Bay came back and said that the *Herman* had been there, but had left for Cape Bering, so I sent word there to see if I could catch the captain. While he was on his way there, however, he heard through the natives of my being at Emma Harbor and on the afternoon of the twenty-first I was delighted to see the *Herman* come steaming in.

I did not need to be told that she was there for me and went aboard at once. The captain greeted me hospitably and made no demur when I told him how anxious I was to be set ashore at Nome as soon as possible. I cannot express too strongly my warm appreciation of the kindness of the captain and his crew, for it meant a considerable delay in his trading voyage and consequent loss to the men who, according to the established custom, were working entirely on shares. He told me that ever since he had been on this coast the weather had been bad. He had got the natives aboard again and again, to trade with them, only to have the wind spring up and make it necessary for him to up-anchor with all speed and put to sea again.

I bade good-by to the baron and to my other kind friends at Emma Harbor and we started for Alaska. The distance across Bering Sea at that point is about 240 miles. When we reached the edge of the ice off Nome on the twenty-fourth we found that we could not steam in near enough to the land for me to get ashore. There was nothing to do but to lie off shore about twelve miles and hope for the ice to break up enough to enable the ship to be worked in nearer the town. There is no harbor at Nome; it is simply an open shore, unsafe for vessels in any kind of bad weather, and conditions have to be exactly right before a ship can venture in. For three days we lay there, while my patience underwent a severe test; all I could do was to read the magazines and gaze at the shore, twelve miles away.

Finally, during the afternoon of the twenty-seventh the captain decided to go to St. Michael's, and we got under way again and steamed across Norton Sound. Early the next morning we arrived off St. Michael's, but on account of thick fog had to anchor and wait. At six P. M. the fog lifted and we steamed in to a point about a mile off shore. The harbor ice was still frozen solid, but we got out a boat and rowed to the edge of the ice and then made our way ashore on foot. It was about eight o'clock in the evening when, with a feeling of great relief, I set foot at last on American soil. Captain Pederson had given me some American clothing to take the place of the furs I had been wearing for so many months. He accompanied me to the wireless station, but when we got there we found that the office was closed.

We walked on in the direction of the town of St. Michael's and on our way I was overjoyed to meet Hugh J. Lee, the United States Marshal. I had met him in Nome the previous summer, which was the first time I had seen him since 1896. He had been with Peary on his Greenland ice-cap trip in 1892 and had been on the *Hope* in 1896 when she touched in at Turnavick on the Labrador, my father's fishing-station, where I was spending a summer vacation. He was astonished to see me in St. Michael's and wanted to know what on earth I was doing there. A few brief explanations put him in touch with the situation and I felt that I was in the hands of a good friend.

Lee took me to the agent of the Northern Commercial Company, which has a large trading-house at St. Michael's, and I was given a good room in the winter hotel where the company's employees are quartered. The summer hotel was closed. Lee and I sat up until late that night, talking over

THE NEWS OF CAPTAIN BARTLETT'S ARRIVAL
AT ST. MICHAEL'S REACHES NOME

the *Karluk's* drift and the subsequent adventures of our ship's company.

Early the next morning I was at the office of the wireless, which is a military station of the Signal Corps of the United States Army. I had very little money and as he had to follow the regulations the sergeant in charge refused to send my message to Ottawa unless I could pay for it. This was an unexpected obstacle. I had travelled a good many hundred miles to reach this spot and I am afraid that I almost lost my patience with the red tape that could stand in the way of a message that had to be sent. About that time Lee came in and explained matters, and the sergeant finally concluded to send the message, which 1 had written:

ST. MICHAEL'S, ALASKA,
May 29, 1914.

Naval Service, Ottawa, Canada:

Karluk ice pressure sank January 11, sixty miles north Herald Island. Preparation made last fall leave ship therefore comfortable on ice. January twenty-first sent first and second mate two sailors with supporting party three months provisions Wrangell Island. Supporting party returned leaving them close Herald Island. They expected land island when ice moved in shore. February fifth Mackay, Murray, Beuchat, Sailor Morris left us using man power pull sledges. Sent again Herald Island three sledges, twenty dogs, pemmican, biscuit, oil. Open water prevented their

landing. Saw no signs men, presumed they gone
Wrangell. Returning left provisions along trail.
Shortly after their return east gale sent us west.
February twenty-fourth I left camp. March
twelfth landed Munro, Williamson, Malloch, Mc-
Kinlay, Mamen, Hadley, Chafe, Templeman,
Maurer, Breddy, Williams, Eskimo family Wran-
gell eighty-six days' supplies each man.

March seventeenth Munro two men fourteen
dogs left for supplies Shipwreck Camp. Plenty
of driftwood game island. March eighteenth I
left island Eskimo landed Siberia fifty miles west
Cape North. May twenty-first Captain Pederson
Whaler *Herman* called for me Emma Harbor
going out of his way whaling to do so. Soundings
meteorological observations dredging kept up continually. Successful. Twelve hundred fathoms
animal life found bottom.

Need funds pay bills contracted Siberia and here.
Wire Northern Commercial Company, San Francisco, five hundred dollars. Instruct them forward
by wire St. Michael's.

BARTLETT, CAPTAIN, C. G. S.

My own special task was done. The responsibility for what remained to be done would be shared
with others; means must be devised for the rescue
of the men on Wrangell Island.

CHAPTER XXIX

WAITING

The days following my arrival at St. Michael's were busy ones for me. My immediate problem was to see what ships were available to make the voyage to Wrangell Island when navigation opened. Not until midsummer would conditions be right, and even then, as we had found in the *Karluk,* the time of open water was likely to be brief and might be cut short at any moment. I received many messages—from my family in Newfoundland, from my friends in Boston and elsewhere, from the press and from the authorities in Ottawa. I even had a telegram from the advertising department of an enterprising American periodical: "Please wire our expense permission to use your picture smoking pipe for tobacco advertisement. What brand do you smoke?"

From Ottawa I received a message expressing the relief of the authorities at news of the *Karluk* —which, I found, had been generally given up for lost, with all on board—and asking for advice and details regarding arrangements for the rescue of the men and the time when ice conditions would allow their being taken off the island.   To this inquiry I replied:

ST. MICHAEL'S, ALASKA,
May 30, 1914.
Hon. G. J. Desbarats,
Naval Service, Ottawa, Canada.

Russian ice-breakers *Taimir* and *Vaigatch* soon make annual exploring trip north coast Siberia. Strongly advise you try arrange Russian Government these vessels relieve men.   Vessels wintered Vladivostock but may have already left for north. Failing this arrangement another Russian ice-breaker *Nadjeshny* lying idle Vladivostock might be obtained.   Another chance United States revenue cutter *Bear* now in Bering Sea.   Possible arrangements United States Government.   If *Bear* goes should seek convoy Russian ice-breakers.   No other available vessels these waters.   My opinion July or early August before ice breaks up around Wrangell though seasons differ.   Plenty bird other animal life island good Eskimo hunter should not suffer food.   I want go relief ships.   Russian ships have wireless can get in touch with them if already at sea.

BARTLETT, CAPTAIN.

The *Bear,* as I have mentioned before, had been one of the ships to rescue the survivors of the Greely expedition thirty years before.   I had never made a trip in her but I knew what kind of ship she was. Built in Scotland in the seventies for the Newfoundland seal-fisheries, she was considered a crack sealer for that period and made many successful voyages.   In 1883 the United States Government

was fitting out an expedition under Commander
Schley to go to the Arctic to relieve Greely and his
men.   The *Bear* and the *Thetis* were all ready to
leave St. John's for their sealing trips, with their
crews and outfits all arranged for.   They were just
the ships for the purpose and the United States
Government bought them, paying, besides a liberal
price for the vessels themselves, the amount of
money that would have been shared by their officers
and men if they had made good sealing trips.
Many people, I have discovered, have supposed
that the ships were given by England; what led to
this supposition was the fact that Queen Victoria
gave the United States the *Alert,* which, with the
Nares Expedition, had spent the winter of 1875-6
at Floe-Berg Beach, Grant Land, somewhat south
of our winter quarters at Cape Sheridan in the
Roosevelt in the winters of 1905-6 and 1908-9.
Will Norman, a relative of mine, from my own
town of Brigus, Newfoundland, went as ice-pilot
of the *Thetis,* on her voyage for the Greely survivors, and Captain Ash, from Trinity Bay, Newfoundland, who afterwards for many years was
master of the Red·Cross boats, plying between St.
John's and New York, was ice-pilot of the *Bear.*
With the quality of the ship in mind, and her past
record, to say nothing of her present work in Alaskan waters, I felt no doubt that the *Bear* would

get through to Wrangell Island if any ship could do so. I had been told, too, that her master, Captain Cochran, was not afraid to put her in the ice, for he had served under that fearless and true-hearted man, the late Captain Jarvis. On the whole, it seemed to me that it would be a matter of singular interest for the *Bear* to rescue the *Karluk* survivors as she had rescued the Greely party thirty years before, on the other side of the continent.

The Russian ships, *Taimir* and *Vaigatch,* also, had fine records. I have already mentioned the success of Captain Vilkitski in the *Taimir* in discovering Nicholas II Land in 1913. I knew that both vessels were similar to the steel ships used in the Newfoundland seal-fisheries and that they were able craft, equipped with powerful engines.

During my stay in St. Michael's I was fortunate in having the skilful treatment of Doctor Fernbaugh, the government surgeon, so that I soon got around again. He was very good to me, making me feel at home and treating me like a brother. The boys at the wireless station were kind enough to give me the back files to read, so that I could get an idea of what had been happening in the world. The agents of the Northern Commercial Company, too, were most hospitable and treated me as one of their own.

When I first reached St. Michael's, the *Bear,*

coming up from San Francisco, was about due in Nome, to bring the mail and take up her regular summer work, the first ship from the "outside" to reach Nome that year. On account of the ice around Nome and the delay of the mail-boat *Victoria* from Seattle, which ordinarily would have brought the mail from Nome to St. Michael's, the *Bear* came in to St. Michael's and landed the mail there. I went on board and Captain Cochran and his officers talked over the plight of the men on Wrangell Island with me and expressed a desire to go to the island and rescue the men. At this time they had not received instructions from Washington regarding the trip, but not long afterwards, while they were on their way over to the Siberian coast, their orders came by wireless to go to the island and to take me with them. It was while the *Bear* was at St. Michael's that I first made the acquaintance of Lord William Percy, the son of the Duke of Northumberland. He was making a summer cruise in the *Bear* to study the ducks of Alaskan waters. He was a master of his subject. My first meeting with him was down in the 'tween-decks of the *Bear,* in a corner among boxes and barrels, surrounded by various kinds of knives, scissors and the other gear necessary to mount birds. He gave me welcome messages from friends of mine whom he had met in Boston and New York.

Later on I was with him on many of his ornitho-logical expeditions and learned a good deal about ducks from him. He could tell at a glance the sex and species of a bird; to the average man, even to many a fairly experienced hunter, a duck is a duck. On the *Bear* I found another ornithologist, an enthusiast named Hershey, who left us later on and went over to the mouth of the Yukon.

The latter part of June I went over to Nome to wait for the *Bear*. I was feeling better all the time, and looked forward to being on my way to Wrangell Island before many weeks.

At Nome I was the guest of Mr. Japhet Linder-berg, mine-owner and operator, who in many ways might be called the Cecil Rhodes of Alaska. There was no limit to his kindness and generosity to me. Though he has made a fortune in gold-mining he works as hard as ever and attends personally to a vast number of details. The forty-two-mile ditch-line that conveys water to his sluices is the result of an idea of his own and he still gives it his personal attention, going over it frequently to see that every-thing is all right. The season is short in Nome and the expense of mining is great; whatever is to be done must be done between the middle of June and the middle of September, and without water very little could be done at all.

On several of his inspection-trips over the line
I had the pleasure of accompanying him. On one
occasion we were joined by Major MacManus,
with whom I had come over by motor-boat from St.
Michael's; the major was on an inspection tour
among the army posts, a typical soldier of the very
best type, alert, vigorous and a great companion.
I believe he could ride a horse forever without getting tired. On this occasion he rode a horse be-
longing to Mr. Linderberg, who rode his own favorite mount, while I rode a horse from the army
post. It was a typical northern summer day, with
bright sunshine and not a breath of air stirring.
The slopes of the distant mountains were
green, and their jagged peaks, with crowns
of perpetual snow, stood out brilliantly against
the clear, blue sky, while in the distance was
the blue haze that I have seen so many times in the
mountains of New England in the early fall before the leaves begin to turn. As we were riding
along we came to a bend and Mr. Linderberg
got off his horse to see how deep the water was
at this particular place. My saddle-girths were
slack, so, while we were waiting for Mr. Linderberg to complete his calculations, I dismounted and
began to tighten them. I had my pipe with me,
so I filled it and lighted up. While I was doing

this the others started on their way; I finished lighting my pipe, mounted my horse and started after
them.

There were many turns in the path and as they
were trotting along I soon lost sight of them.   I
was enjoying myself, however, and let my horse
walk along at his leisure, while I let my eyes wander
gratefully over the scene before me; no sound was
to be heard but the singing of the birds.   I just
gave the horse his head and sat or lolled in the
saddle, smoking and day-dreaming.

I was rudely recalled from dreamland by something altogether realistic, a wheelbarrow which was
turned bottom-up on the path.   The horse saw it
before I did, evidently, and was so violently pre-
judiced against it that he tried at once to avoid it,
without considering whether I disliked wheelbar-
rows or not, for the first thing I knew I was in the
icy waters of the ditch, which at that point was
six or eight feet deep.   My cap floated away at
once, but I kept my pipe in my mouth and when I
came to the surface still had it.

I was soon out of the water, of course, and then
was seized with an uncontrollable fit of laughter.
I just stood and laughed and laughed and laughed
again.   The horse ran only a short distance and
then stopped and waited for me.   I took off my
clothes and wrung them out; when I put them on

again, remounted and started along the path, I
felt quite warm and dry before long, at least on
the left side where the sunshine pelted down. I
did not hurry the horse but let him walk along
slowly until, by the time I came up with the others,
I looked dry enough on my port side.

The major heard me laughing as I came near
them and wondered quite naturally what was the
matter with me to be so uncontrollably mirthful,
but I kept my right side carefully turned away from
them and they were none the wiser. Again and
again, as we rode along, I would go off into a fit
of laughter until finally, when we dismounted at
the house of one of the men who looked after the
ditch-line, I took pity on their curiosity and told
them what had happened to me.

It was now about midnight and the sun had just
set behind the mountain peaks so Mr. Linderberg
said that we would do a little trout-fishing. We
started out and I was eager to see what luck we
should have but in a very short time I completely
lost interest in the sport, the mosquitoes were
swarming about us in such clouds. They were
large, well-built and utterly unterrified by any
word or act on my part, though I am not conscious
of omitting any, and the Recording Angel was busy
for a short time. It was only for a short time,
however, for, though my companions were appar-

ently untroubled and even took a curious kind of pleasure in my struggles, I was glad to acknowledge myself beaten by the far-famed Alaska mosquito. I was literally a sight, my face, neck and hands red and swollen the next morning, whereas the major and my host showed no evidences that there had been any mosquitoes in their neighborhood.

In the mountainous country near Nome there are often sudden showers, accompanied by very high winds, so whenever we were out riding we always carried our oilskins strapped behind our saddles. On one of our rides we saw a storm coming up but hoped that it would pass us by; the tail-end of it struck us, however, with a deluge of rain and a high wind. I had not bothered to get off my horse to put on my coat and when the storm was upon us I unloosed the coat from behind my saddle and started to put it on. Just as I got my arms in the sleeves the wind took it and whirled it out into a kind of balloon. This frightened the horse and he turned suddenly around and started for the water. Then he as suddenly changed his mind and tore madly down over the outside edge of the embankment while my arms were seesawing back and forth as I tried to get them through the coatsleeves. After a while I managed to get one arm out, holding on by gripping my knees to the horse's body, and as the horse started for some low trees I slid off without a scratch, though I did not deserve any such luck. The others came up very much disturbed, for they were sure that I would fall off among the boulders and be killed.

The time that I spent at Nome, though I was naturally very anxious for the moment to come when we should be on our way to get the men on the island, was made to pass pleasantly by the many good friends whom I made there. I lived at the Golden Gate Hotel but took my meals at the Log Cabin Club. The club had a Japanese chef named Charlie, who was really a wonder; one dined as well there as at any good hotel in San Francisco. The club is the great meeting-place in Nome and many were the lively political discussions we had there.

I could fill a book with descriptions of the interesting people I met in Nome. There was Doctor Neuman, a great student of the Alaskan Eskimo, and the author of important books about them, and more than that a man who has done them a great deal of good and is greatly beloved by them. There was Jim Swartzwell, the proprietor of the Golden Gate Hotel, a typical, open-hearted, Alaskan sour-dough; no man or woman ever came to him for assistance and went away empty-handed. I saw the house where Rex Beach lived in Nome and met the originals of many of the characters in his stories, who were some of them story-books in themselves.

CHAPTER XXX

From time to time there came rumors of how close the season was and how much ice there was about the coast. This was disquieting. I had told the captains of the vessels that from time to time left Nome for the northern waters, walrus-hunting or trading, about the men on Wrangell Island and had asked them, if they got anywhere near the island, to take a look around. By the first week in July I began to get more and more uneasy and anxious to get started. The *Bear* had been in the north and reported on her return that the ice was heavy and still closely packed, and the walrus-hunter *Kit* came back from north of Bering Strait with the same story. Such news was not at all reassuring, though I knew that the ice could be broken up in a few hours' time just as it could form in an equally short interval. The tenth of August, I reckoned, should see us at Wrangell Island; the men would not really be expecting me much before that time.

The *Bear* finally got away, with me on board, on July 13. She had a number of calls to make on her

way north, for in addition to being the mail-boat,
she had to bring help to the needy, act as a kind
of travelling law-court, carry school-teachers and
missionaries around from place to place and make
herself generally useful.   It was a great relief to
me to be really doing something at last, after so
many weeks of inaction.   My thoughts were constantly on the castaways and I wondered how things
had been going with them since the middle of
March.

We had a pleasant ship's company.   I slept in
the captain's cabin.   On the port side in a hammock was the Reverend Doctor Hoar, who was accompanying us as far as his mission station at
Point Hope.   In another hammock was Mr.
Shields, the Alaskan Superintendent of Educa-
tion, an able young man who has done wonders
with the means at his disposal to foster the spirit
of thrift among the Eskimo in their reindeer-herd-
ing.   He knows every nook and cranny from
Nome to Point Barrow and has won the respect
and admiration of the Eskimo everywhere.   On
the starboard side were Hershey and E. Swift
Train, who was taking motion-pictures and gathering material for the use of schools.

Just across the way was the wardroom and a
finer set of men than the officers of the *Bear* I never
met.   They had the latchstring always out.   I was

privileged to visit the chart-room at any time and had the rare opportunity of learning from Lieutenant Dempwolf, the navigating officer, much about Alaskan and Siberian waters. It was fine to feel a good ship like the *Bear* under one and worth while seeing others navigate. A lot of merchant-marine men would be greatly benefited by a trip on a revenue-cutter.

Our first stop was Reindeer Station at St. Lawrence Island. Then we went to other stations on St. Lawrence Island, with supplies for the schools there, and then on to St. Lawrence Bay on the Siberian coast, to Lütke Island. From there we went to Emma Town and picked up Lord Percy, who had been collecting birds at Lütke Island and had come up with a native in a skin-boat. At Emma Town I again met the Mr. Caraieff who had taken me to Emma Harbor; his brother had gone to Vladivostock. Here I paid the money I owed. Some of the dogs I had left were still here but only two of them were any good; the others were still not rested enough to be of use. They were offered me again but I told my kind friends to keep them if they could get any good out of them. When I had been there before the snow had been piled high over everything. How different it all looked on this beautiful July afternoon! When Lord Percy had picked up his things at Emma Town we

steamed along the coast to East Cape, and then to
Ugelen, near by. From here we went across to
Teller, on the Alaskan coast, and visited various
settlements.

At Reindeer Station, at Port Clarence, I met
again the Reverend Mr. Brevick, the missionary in
charge, whom I had met the previous year when we
were there in the *Karluk;* he again treated me
royally. We waited here while Mr. Shields and
Lieutenant Dempwolf, in the steam-launch, visited
some of the settlements farther up the bay.

It was while we were in Kotzebue Sound on
August 4 that we heard over the wireless that war
had been declared between Germany and France
and then between Germany and England. It may
be imagined what an effect such an amazing piece
of news, coming to us in such a detached way in
so remote a corner of the world, had upon us; at
first, of course, we had difficulty in believing it,
but there seemed to be no doubt of its accuracy,
so Lord Percy, who was an officer in the British
army, left us to get back to England as soon as
possible. I have heard from him since of his life in
the trenches. He is one of the many men of the
"nobility and gentry" who have uncomplainingly
done their duty for their country. Mr. Shields
went ashore at Kotzebue with Lord Percy, for

somewhere in the vicinity he was to establish a new Eskimo village. We went on to Point Hope, where Doctor Hoar left us.

At Point Hope I again met Kataktovick, who had been brought over from East Cape by Captain Pederson in the *Herman*. I paid him his wages, as a member of the *Karluk* expedition, and gave him a complete outfit of clothing which the Canadian Government was providing for each man of the party. He would have liked to go with us on the trip to Wrangell Island, if it had been possible. He was feeling well, he said, and from the looks of things seemed about to be married.

From Point Hope we headed for Point Barrow. Off Icy Cape we met the first ice and from there on it was a constant fight to make our way along; evidently it was not an open season. Accompanying us were the *King and Winge*, a walrus-hunter and trader, managed by Mr. Olaf Swenson, and a Canadian schooner, loaded with supplies for the mounted police at Herschel Island. The schooner had a big deckload and was very heavy in the water. She was not sheathed and had no stem-plates, and was evidently not at all adapted for ice work. In fact, it seemed doubtful to me whether she ever would reach Point Barrow. The *King and Winge*, on the other hand, was just in the right ballast for bucking the ice; besides being small, she was short for her beam and was quick to answer the helm.

The ice through which we were making our toilsome way was not so heavy as it was closely packed. It was great to see the good old *Bear* charging and recharging, twisting and turning; being heavy in the water she was able, with her great momentum, to smash off points and corners of the ice and make her way through it. I should have been delighted to be in the crow's-nest, for steering such a ship through the ice is not unlike driving a big automobile through a crowded thoroughfare; this time, however, I was a passenger.

Near Wainwright Inlet we found a large four-masted schooner ashore. The *Bear* tried in vain to get her off; she was fast aground and heavily loaded. The only thing that could be done was to take her cargo out of her. While we were standing by, the ice began to close in and we had to turn round and steam south in a hurry, leaving our big line with the schooner. When we got back again some days later she had been floated all right.

We reached Point Barrow on the evening of the twenty-first of August. Here I found McConnell, who had come in a small schooner from the eastward. He told me all about what had happened to Stefansson after the *Karluk* had been blown offshore by the storm which began her drift in the September of the previous year.

The party that left the *Karluk* on September 20, 1913, as I have related before, consisted of Stefansson, Jenness, Wilkins, McConnell and the two Eskimo boys who had come aboard at Point Hope, Panyurak and Asatshak. They had with them two sledges and twelve dogs and equipment sufficient for the purpose which took them ashore, a two weeks' caribou hunt in the country back of Beechey Point to provide the ship's company with needed fresh meat for the winter, which it seemed likely would be spent with the ship frozen in at that point. It took them, McConnell said, two days to work their way in over the ice to one of the Jones Islands, about six miles northwest of Beechey Point. When they finally reached the island they found that the ice between them and the mainland was not safe for travelling, so while they were waiting for it to freeze more solidly, Stefansson decided to send him and Asatshak back to the *Karluk* for some things they wanted.

That night, however, the storm that sent us drifting off shore came up and it was clearly not safe for them to go out on the sea-ice for the present. At the end of the three days' storm the sea was clear on the outside and the ship was nowhere to be seen. Whether she was free at last and on

her way eastward towards Herschel Island or had
been blown westward into the waters north of Point
Barrow they did not know.   It was impossible for
them to get ashore until the twenty-eighth, when
they reached Beechey Point.   They stayed in this
vicinity for several days and Stefansson did a little
caribou hunting without success.   The Eskimo
became alarmed because there was not a larger
amount of food, for they were civilized Eskimo
and unused to living off the country, so finally on
the third of October the party started westward towards Point Barrow.   They made the march of
175 miles in nine days.

They stayed at Point Barrow for some time to
procure fur clothing and provisions for the party,
as well as a sledge and a dog-team.   On November 8 they started east again.   The latter part of
the month they reached Cape Halkett, where they
met an experienced Eskimo hunter named Angupkanna, otherwise called "the Stammerer," who told
them that early in October he saw a ship in the ice
off shore and through his telescope could see her
distinctly.   Stefansson was sure that she was the
Karluk, a ship with which the Eskimo was well
acquainted from her whaling days.   Angupkanna
told them that he watched her for three or four
hours and then fog settled down for three days, at
the end of which time he saw her no more.

Leaving Jenness at Cape Halkett to make some ethnological studies, Stefansson, Wilkins and McConnell went on to the east once more and the middle of December reached Flaxman Island, where they found Leffingwell, who had come up on the *Mary Sachs* to finish some work he had begun the year before. He was wintering alone, though an Eskimo family was living not far away from him.

Leaving Leffingwell on December 14, they reached the winter quarters of the southern party at Collinson Point, thirty miles to the eastward, on the evening of the same day. Here they spent the winter. Stefansson made a journey later on still farther to the east with a member of the southern party to Herschel Island and Fort Mackenzie, to make plans for the journey which he was to undertake in the spring over the ice to the north of Martin Point in search of new land. In the latter part of February McConnell made a trip to Point Barrow for the mail, returning to Martin Point not long after Stefansson, with a party of seven men, had started north over the ice on March 22. With a companion McConnell overtook them the next day and they travelled on for more than two weeks, until, on April 6 they reached the edge of the continental shelf, discovered by Mikkelson and Leffingwell in the *Duchess of Bedford* expedition in 1907. At this point Stefansson sent the supporting party back, and went on to the northward with six dogs, a sledge and forty days' supplies, together with two rifles and 360 rounds of ammunition. He had with him two companions, Storker Storkerson, who had been mate of the *Duchess of Bedford* and had been living as a hunter and trapper at various places along the shore since the date of the Mikkelson expedition, and Ole Anderson, another experienced man. Stefansson intended to go on for fifteen days' march before turning back and hoped to do by ice travel what the *Karluk* had been prevented from doing—to discover new land along the 141st Meridian.[1] Stefansson had not since been heard from, McConnell said, but there should be plenty of bear and seal for his party to subsist on and it was likely that in any event they could make their way to Banks Land.

At Point Barrow, too, in the *Bear* we found several shipwrecked crews waiting for a chance to go south. We landed the mails and the various other things we had brought for the station there and then, finding that, as I have related, the schooner that we had found aground had floated, we headed at last for Wrangell Island. I was becoming more and more anxious to get there and

1 Stefansson was successful in his quest for new land and, in 1915 and 1916, reported his discoveries.

THE CAMP AT RODGERS HARBOR, WRANGELL ISLAND

"Following their instructions to divide into smaller parties, for general harmony and larger hunting areas, Mamen, Malloch and Templeman . . . went down . . . to Rodgers Harbor. Here they erected a tent." *See page 319*

hoped that meanwhile the Russian ships or one of
the walrus-hunting boats had been there and taken
off the men.   It was getting late and before many
weeks the ice might close in around the island and
render it inaccessible to a ship, but it was not altogether this danger alone that worried me but also
the feeling that the longer the men were kept on
the island the greater would be their suspense and
the harder it would be for them to keep up their
spirits.   Of course, until some one came to rescue
them they would not know whether I had ever succeeded in reaching the Siberian coast or not.
Every day of this suspense must be telling on them
and bringing them face to face with the thought
that they might have to spend another winter on
the island, an experience which would be likely to
kill them all.   So altogether these days had been
nightmares to me, the more so because naturally
under the circumstances I was not in a position to
do anything to hasten matters.   The *Bear* had her
own work to do, of course, and only a limited season to do it in.   My feeling of relief at being at
last on the way to the goal of all my thought and
effort may be imagined.

We left on August 23, with a fresh north-north-
east wind behind us, and straightened her out for
Rodgers Harbor.   The harder it blew the better
I liked it, for our voyage would be so much the

quicker. The only thing I was afraid of was that we might get thick fog or snow and be delayed indefinitely.

On the afternoon of the twenty-fourth we met the ice, large loose pieces similar to the ice I had seen off the southern end of the island on my way across with Kataktovick. The weather became hazy and then we had the fog that I was fearing. All the square sails were taken in and we slowly steamed to the northwest. At eight P. M. the engines were stopped and the ship was headed east half south. During the afternoon countless birds were seen, denoting the proximity of land; it seemed as if we must soon be there. During the next day the ship worked slowly towards the island again and at ten A. M. we met a lot more large, loose ice. We were now between fifteen and twenty miles from the island and if the fog had lifted should have been there in a short time and had the men off. We had about ninety tons of coal in the bunkers. All day long on the twenty-fifth it was thick, but we could see a mile or so ahead and were still going along easily, just keeping the ship under steerageway. Finally, at eight o'clock in the evening, the engines were stopped, the ship was hove hull to and allowed to drift. The next day the wind had hauled to the north-northwest and sent us drifting away from the island, towards the Siberian shore. At 4.12 A. M. on the morning of the twenty-seventh, Captain Cochran decided to go back to Nome for a new supply of coal.   My feelings at this moment can be easily imagined.   The days that followed were days to try a man's soul.   In fact, until the final rescue of the men, I spent such a wretched time as I had never had in my life.

We did not return directly to Nome but called at Cape Serdze to make an attempt to find out about a missing boat owned by Dr. Hoar, which had broken away from Point Hope the previous fall.   Mr. Wall was away.   I went ashore with Lieutenant Dempwolf and tried to find out whether the Russian ships had been to Wrangell Island. I learned from Corrigan that a Russian ship had passed west but that he had not seen her coming back; it turned out that she had gone up to Koliuchin with coal and was not one of the ice-breakers. I gave Corrigan some pipes and tobacco.

From Cape Serdze we went on to East Cape and I went ashore here to see if I could learn anything about the Russian ice-breakers at Mr. Caraieff's.   Mr. Carpendale told me that the report was that the *Vaigatch* had been within ten miles of Wrangell Island on August 4, when she got a wireless message with news of the war and was ordered

CHAPTER XXXI

THE RESCUE FROM WRANGELL ISLAND

On August 30, at half past seven in the evening, we anchored off Nome. Early the next morning a lighter came alongside with coal but a fresh southwest wind sprang up while we were loading and we had to put to sea, leaving about five tons of coal still aboard the lighter. By eleven o'clock the wind had moderated and we were able to come back to our anchorage again. I paid a call on Mr. Linderberg, who was financially interested in the company supplying us with coal, and he took pains to see that things were pushed forward as fast as possible. Just before dark another gale sprang up and we were forced to put to sea again. By noon the next day, September 2, it was safe for us to return and the lighter was soon alongside. We finished with her by four o'clock the next morning but on account of the fact that in the blow several lighters loaded with coal had been driven aground on the beach and the mail-boat *Victoria,* from Seattle, also had to discharge freight and needed lighters, there was no other lighter of coal to take the place of the one with which we had just finished.

I had luncheon with Mr. Linderberg. He was well aware of my extreme uneasiness about the continued delay and told me that he had decided to send the *Corwin* to Wrangell Island after the men; she had formerly been in the revenue cutter service and, as I have already noted, had made an interesting trip to Wrangell in the early eighties. While ashore to see Mr. Linderberg I ran across Mr. Swenson, of the *King and Winge*, in Mr. Goggin's store, a great rendezvous in Nome, and learned from him that he was about to start for the Siberian coast on a trading and walrus-hunting trip. I asked him, if he went anywhere near Wrangell Island, to call and see if the men had been taken off and he promised that he would do so. I sent a telegram to Ottawa to let the authorities know that the *Corwin* was going to try to reach the island and that the *King and Winge* would be in that vicinity, too, and would call there if she could.

The *Bear* finished her coaling at nine o'clock on the morning of the fourth and then had to spend the next few hours taking on water. At one o'clock an onshore wind sprang up and I went off to the ship. We got away at ten minutes past two but spent all the next day at Port Clarence, looking for water. I was feeling easier in my mind now because I felt sure that Mr. Swenson would go straight to the island, whether the *Bear* ever got there or not.

Daylight on the sixth found us off Cape York. We were going along with a fair wind and all sail set. Early in the afternoon we rounded East Cape; so far we were doing well. The wind came dead ahead in the late afternoon. By dark we were abreast of Cape Serdze. The next morning the wind was north-northwest and the sea smooth, a thing which told us clearly that the ice was near. All day long conditions remained the same and at quarter of eight in the evening we were not surprised to see the ice. We were 131 miles from Rodgers Harbor. We lay near the edge of the ice and waited for daylight.

As soon as dawn broke September 8, we went on full speed ahead, through the loose ice; some distance away, on our port bow, we could see that the ice was close-packed. By early afternoon we had made more than fifty miles and were about seventy-five miles from our goal. Luncheon was just finished and I was standing in the chart-room, when we saw a schooner dead ahead, running before the wind. The glasses were soon trained on her and we saw that she was the *King and Winge*. I hoped and was inclined to believe that she had been to the island, or she would hardly be coming back so soon. Then I began to fear that perhaps she had broken her propeller and was now taking advantage of the favoring wind to put for Bering Strait and Alaska.

I watched her as she drew nearer and nearer; then she hove to and we were soon alongside. I looked sharply at the men on her deck; her own crew was fairly large, but soon I could pick out Munro and McKinlay and Chafe, and of course the Eskimo family, and I knew that our quest was over. A boat was lowered from the *Bear,* with Lieutenant Miller in charge; I obtained permission from the captain to go along and was soon on board the *King and Winge,* among the *Karluk* party.

"All of you here?" was my first question.

McKinlay was the spokesman. "No," he answered; "Malloch and Mamen and Breddy died on the island."

There was nothing to be said. I had not really expected to see the mate's party or the Mackay party, for I had long since ceased to believe that there was any reasonable chance that they could have got through to a safe place, but though it was hard to be forced to what appeared the inevitable conclusion in their case, it was an especially sad and bitter blow to learn that three of the men whom I had seen arrive at Wrangell Island had thus reached safety only to die.

THE RESCUE OF THE PARTY AT WARING POINT, WRANGELL ISLAND

"The rescue, both here and at Rodgers Harbor, was effected just in time."

None of the three could well be spared. Breddy had been a careful and efficient worker in all the struggles we had gone through since the storm had carried us away in the previous September. Mamen was a great companion, indoors or out; he especially excelled in all athletic sports that demanded fearlessness and endurance, and he was, besides this, a devoted and helpful associate. At one time, in fact, I had had it in mind to send him to the Siberian coast with Kataktovick in my stead, if the injury to his knee-cap had not incapacitated him, and, if he had been able to start on such a journey, I feel confident that he would have made it or died in the attempt. Malloch was an ideal man for an exploring expedition like ours, brought face to face by circumstances with conditions that were calculated to test to the utmost a man's real nature, for he was not only fully equipped in his own special field of science but beyond all that he was one of the most self-sacrificing men with whom it has ever been my lot to be thrown into intimate contact. If his task for the moment happened to be something connected with his own work as a scientist, he performed it as a matter of course, and if it happened to be sweeping the floor or doing any other odd job that needed to be done, he did that equally as a matter of course, without the slightest thought of self or any other idea in mind except to be as useful as possible to his companions.

I shook hands all around with our party and then with Mr. Swenson and Captain Jochimsen, the brave skipper of the *King and Winge,* and thanked them in the name of the Canadian Government for rescuing the men. Then I asked Mr. Swenson's permission to have the *Karluk* people transferred to the *Bear.* There they could receive the medical attention that they needed, for there was no doctor on the *King and Winge;* there was, too, no reason now why Mr. Swenson should not continue the walrus-hunt that he had postponed to go to Wrangell Island for the men of the *Karluk.* McConnell, also, who was on the *King and Winge,* came on board the *Bear* with the rest.

To get the whole party and their few possessions over to the *Bear* took about an hour. Then we said good-by to the *King and Winge* and steamed in the direction of Herald Island to make a search for the mate's and the doctor's parties, though there was no likelihood of seeing any traces of them. At dark, owing to the ice, the engines were kept working easy ahead; at eight o'clock the next morning, September 9, we were twelve miles from Herald Island. The ice kept us from getting any nearer, and after we had done what we could to find a way through, Captain Cochran decided to go back to

Nome. Mr. Swenson had already taken the *King and Winge* as near Herald Island as he could get, without seeing any signs of human life, and months before, shortly after my departure with Kataktovick for Siberia, McKinlay and Munro had made their way across the ice in the direction of Herald Island and had got near enough to see that no one was there. Later on, as I afterwards learned, the *Corwin,* on the trip on which, as he had promised, Mr. Linderberg sent her, cruised all around Herald Island without seeing any evidences that any one had been there. It was as certain as anything could be that both parties had long since perished, but it was very hard for me to give them up, men with whom I had spent so many months, men with the future still before them.

From the vicinity of Herald Island, the *Bear* headed for Cape Serdze and at six o'clock the next morning we anchored off Mr. Wall's place. Mr. Wall was still away and we did not stop long but were soon steaming down the coast on the way to our next stop, Cape Prince of Wales.

I did not attempt to press the men for an account of what had happened on the island. They had been through a long period of suspense and were entitled to a rest, so it seemed the kindest thing to let the story come out spontaneously as time went on. McKinlay told me part of it and gradually further details appeared, as they came out in general conversation.

Kataktovick and I, as I have already related, left the island on March 18. The Munro party, starting the day before for Shipwreck Camp, made their way with comparatively little difficulty over the ice until they had crossed the great pressure-ridge that had held us up so long on the way in. Not far on the other side they came to open water, so they had to return to the island.

Various trips were afterwards made out on the ice, on one of which Williams froze his great toe so badly that there was nothing to do but to ampu-tate it, to save the foot and possibly further com-plications. Perhaps many people would have pre-ferred to risk one danger at a time, rather than be operated on with the means at hand. Williamson was the surgeon; he had shown his natural deft-ness, as I have mentioned before, by his care of Mamen's dislocated knee-cap at Shipwreck Camp. His instruments consisted of a pocket-knife and a pair of tin-shears. Perhaps no more painful and primitive operation was ever performed in the Arctic, though the whaling captains have fre-quently had to exercise a rough and ready surgery, whether it was possible to live up to the require-ments of Listerism or not. Williamson did his work well, and his patient did his part with rare grit, so that the result was a success.

Following their instructions to divide into smaller parties, for general harmony and larger hunting areas, Mamen, Malloch and Templeman left the main party on Icy Spit and went down around the southeastern shore of the island to Rodgers Harbor. Here they erected a tent and planned to build a house of driftwood, a plan which on account of circumstances they were never able to carry into effect. Towards the end of May Malloch and Mamen became ill with nephritis and died, Malloch first and Mamen only a few days later. Templeman was thus left alone, until he was joined by Munro and Maurer, who stayed with him until the rescue. They lived on birds' eggs and seal and, later in the summer, on some Arctic foxes which fortunately came their way.

During the early spring the party at Icy Spit were fortunate in killing polar bear, which gave them fresh meat. As the season advanced they moved down the coast to Waring Point, where they found conditions more favorable for getting birds than on the barren levels of Icy Spit. Here they pitched their tents again and took up a regular routine of life. Hadley, McKinlay, Kerdrillo, Keruk and the two children occupied one tent and

Williamson, Chafe, Williams and Breddy the other. Breddy accidentally shot himself later on, making the third death on the island. Hadley and Kerdrillo hunted daily and as the season advanced they were able to get seal and duck, which gave sufficient food after the supplies that we had brought from Shipwreck Camp had become exhausted the first week in June. It was never possible to get a very large supply of food ahead at any one time, and as the summer wore on and they heard nothing from me they faced the prospect of another winter with misgivings. Hadley and Kerdrillo fashioned a rude Eskimo kayak, by making a framework of driftwood and stretching sealskins over it, and Kerdrillo made good use of this in hunting seal after the ice had broken up.

Both at Rodgers Harbor and at Waring Point the anxiety as to the possibility of our not having made a safe crossing to Siberia to bring help increased as the time went on. It required no undue exercise of the imagination on my part to realize the intense relief which the men felt when, on the morning of the seventh of September, the sound of a steam whistle came across the water to those in the tent at Rodgers Harbor and the party from the *King and Winge* came ashore. This party included Mr. Swenson and members of his own force, together with Eskimo walrus hunters, whom he had

MAKING THE KAYAK ON WRANGELL ISLAND

"Hadley and Kerdrillo fashioned a rude Eskimo kayak, by making a framework of driftwood and stretching sealskins over it, and Kerdrillo made good use of this in hunting seal after the ice had broken up."

taken aboard at East Cape and who had brought the rescue party ashore in their oomiak, and Burt McConnell, who had come up on the *King and Winge* from Nome. Reunited with these other members of the original ship's company, McConnell was now able to tell them of his trip ashore with Stefansson in the previous September and briefly how Kataktovick and I had fared in making our trip to Siberia.

The rescuers helped the rescued to gather together the few possessions of value or interest at the camp and then, leaving a notice for any other ship that might come to see about the men, all hands were soon on board the *King and Winge,* enjoying the luxury of a bath, clean clothes and an ample breakfast. The tent was left standing as it was, but the British flag that had flown so long at half-mast was taken with the rescued men.

With the Rodgers Harbor party safe aboard, the *King and Winge* steamed to Waring Point. On account of the ice they were unable to get nearer than two miles from shore. Swenson and his party, again accompanied by McConnell, went towards the shore over the ice; Kerdrillo came out to meet them. Escorted by him they covered the rest of the distance to the shore, several of the others rushing out over the ice to meet them. It was found that if it had not been for the snow-

storm which was already growing severe the whole
party would have migrated that very day to a point
on the north side of the island where, if they had
to stay through another winter, as seemed not unlikely, they would have a fresh supply of driftwood to draw on. Their camp at Waring Point
was in bad shape. Their tents were wearing out,
their food supply was scanty and they had only
forty rounds of ammunition left with which to provide themselves with food during the coming winter.
To save their cartridges they had lived as far as
possible on birds' eggs, fish which they caught
through the ice and gulls which they obtained by
angling for them on the cliffs with hook and line,
a form of bird-hunting without a shot-gun. The
rescue, both here and at Rodgers Harbor, was
effected just in time.

Leaving a message for whatever ship might follow them here, the Waring Point party joined their
companions from Rodgers Harbor on the *King
and Winge* and the rescue was complete. The
little Eskimo girl brought on board the black cat
which had already had so many vicissitudes that
it was a wonder that it had any of its nine lives still
left to draw on. Here, as at Rodgers Harbor,
the tents were left standing. The party brought
with them the three surviving dogs,—all that were
left out of the twenty that were still living when

we had started for Siberia—and three puppies.

The *King and Winge* steamed towards Herald Island, as I have previously said, but though she kept alongshore for miles she was prevented by the ice-floes from getting very near and finally, to make sure not to be frozen in for the winter, Mr. Swenson decided to set his course for Nome. The weary and anxious *Karluk* survivors enjoyed the food that was hospitably placed before them and the opportunity to bathe and put on clean clothes. The beards that adorned their faces came off and it was a greatly transformed company that I observed from the deck of the *Bear* the next afternoon.

We reached Nome on the *Bear,* September 13. Our arrival aroused great excitement, even though shipwrecked mariners from the Arctic are not altogether a novelty in Nome. The rescue was more than ordinarily a matter of local interest and pride because of the number of men and ships concerned in it that were well known all through that part of Alaska.

The hospitality of the Alaskan is unstinted, as I had already had occasion to find out, but it seemed to me best to keep the men on board the *Bear* for a day or two, for in their reduced state they would be more than usually susceptible to contagious diseases. It would be the irony of fate for them to survive six months of semi-starvation and then fall victim to some ailment of the civilization to which they had so longed to return. To walk in shoes again, too, after so many months of wearing skin-boots, would be painful for a while. After a few days however, they had improved so much that I let them go ashore; they realized the necessity of being careful and had no trouble. Kerdrillo and his family, too, went ashore at Nome, to start on their way home to the North.

It was marvellous how quickly the men picked up in health and strength. On account of frostbite Chafe and Williams were under the doctor's care, though they were otherwise in good shape. The sickest man was Templeman; he could not have survived many days longer. Munro, McKinlay and Hadley, who was in his fifty-eighth year, were all in good condition and would probably have lived through another winter.

We were in Nome until the nineteenth; on that day we headed for the south, our first stop St. Michael's. It seemed advisable to keep the men on the *Bear,* instead of transferring them to any other vessel; there were no mail-boats leaving for the "outside," and the men were warm and comfortable and well cared for. While on our way to St. Michael's we heard by wireless of the stranding of the *Corwin* off Cape Douglas; she was on her way from Wrangell Island to Nome, having heard by

Munro   Hadley   Captain   Keruk   McKinlay   Chafe   Williams
Williamson   Bartlett   Helen
Templeman   Mugpi   Kerdrillo   Maurer

THE *KARLUK* SURVIVORS ON BOARD THE *BEAR*

her wireless that the men had been safely taken
off. About eight o'clock in the morning we came
within sight of her. On account of the broken bottom we could not get nearer than a half mile from
her, so a boat was lowered and the third lieutenant
went on board. The *Bear* lent some of her
crew to help lighten the *Corwin;* then we went on
to the reindeer settlement at Port Clarence for
water. Late in the afternoon on the twenty-
third we reached the *Corwin* again and our men
were returned to us; she was floated a short time
later.

The next day we returned to Nome to get the
Eskimo who belonged on King Island. They had
come to Nome in their large skin-boats a month or
two earlier to sell the great variety of articles that
they are in the habit of carving from the tusks of
the walrus; it is really remarkable what they can
carve in this way: ships, cribbage-boards, houses,
models of men, women and children, etc. The deck
of the *Bear* had the appearance of the first of
May—moving day. These Eskimo had come to
Nome, of course, in the summer; now the season
was getting late and the weather was variable, so
that they did not want to take any chances. And,
indeed, why should they? The *Bear* was there and
the wires were tapped to Washington; furthermore,
Nome did not care to have a couple of hundred

Eskimo on its hands during the winter, so the easiest way out of the difficulty was to get the *Bear* to take them aboard and carry them to their home at King Island, seventy miles away. When we reached there we found that the Eskimo lived in clefts in the rocky cliffs; they were cliff-dwellers. It was a dreary view that met our eyes that cold, windy September morning, but the Eskimo were delighted for to them it was home.

Leaving King Island we called at the school-master's at St. Lawrence Island, to leave mail and provisions from Nome. The latter were badly needed, for short rations had been the order of the day for some time. Steaming around the western end of the island through a smooth sea under brilliant sunshine, we were at last definitely bound south.

With St. Matthew's Island a-beam, the next morning, our wireless reported that all the boats from the *Tahoma* had been picked up; we had heard the S. O. S. call from the *Tahoma* a day or so before. As we afterward learned, the *Cordova,* anchored in the roadstead at Nome, had picked up the *Tahoma's* call and had gone to her assistance. The *Tahoma* had struck an uncharted shoal about a hundred miles south of Agattu Island, one of the western Aleutians, and had become a total loss. The officers and crew had reached land in the ship's boats and were picked up later by the *Cordova* and the *Patterson*.

During the twenty-ninth we were held back by a strong southeast gale, but the following day the wind moderated and on the morning of October first we tied up at the dock at Unalaska, which at the present time is the base where the revenue-cutters get their coal and other supplies. The coal comes from Australia and costs twelve or thirteen dollars a ton. The officer in charge of the station here was Captain Reynolds, who had been a lieutenant on the *Corwin* when she visited Herald Island in the eighties; he read me his diary where he told about their landing on the island and climbing to the top and said that no one could live there and that it was accessible in only one place.

The *Bear* had to stay at Unalaska for several days to have her boilers overhauled. We passed the time in trout-fishing, chiefly, and also climbed Ballyhoo, a thing which every officer in the revenue-cutter service must do. There is a book placed at the summit and every one who climbs the mountain has to sign his name in the book. I went up with Lieutenants Barker and Dempwolf. Lieutenant Kendall and I had some good ptarmigan-shooting in that vicinity.

While we were here McKinlay became ill and had to go to the Jesse Lee Hospital, where he was soon restored to health. I was glad that he was all right, for in circumstances calculated to show men in their true colors I had formed a high opinion of his efficiency and courage. One of the younger members of the expedition and a man of scholarly disposition—he had been a teacher—he showed no lack of grit in an emergency. In such careful transactions as the checking over and dividing up of supplies, I found him of great assistance. He had a good understanding of human nature—perhaps his experience as a schoolmaster had given him that—and I relied on him to preserve harmony if any question should arise among the different groups on Wrangell Island. In all difficulties he was the cool and canny Scot. Of the six scientists left on the *Karluk* after the departure of Stefansson, McKinlay was the sole survivor.

About this time the Revenue-cutter *Manning* was sent to Scotch Cap, Unimak Island, to bring back a lighthouse-keeper who was very ill. The *Manning* anchored off the lighthouse and sent a boat for the keeper. There was a strong tide running but the boat reached the lighthouse safely and started back with the keeper, when it was capsized and the ship's doctor was drowned. We all felt his loss keenly because we had got well acquainted with him while the vessels had been in port together.

At Unalaska I met Captain Miller, of the *Patterson,* the Coast and Geodetic Survey boat, which had been doing a great deal of work that season off the south entrance of the Unimak Pass. He was a very clever man and as I was much interested in his work, we spent a good many hours together; not so very many months later he was to be drowned on the *Lusitania,* in the course of the war whose first unbelievable rumblings we still scarcely heard.

On the afternoon of October 14, with the long homeward pennant flying, we cast off from the pier at Unalaska and steamed south on the last leg of the long journey we had travelled since the June day the year before when we had first left for the north. The voyage south was uneventful and on October 24, 1914, the *Bear* landed us once more at the navy yard at Esquimault.

The next day, under the instructions of the Canadian Government, I paid off the men; soon they had started for their homes, while I left for Ottawa to make my final report of the last voyage of the *Karluk.*

THE END